THE
RED WINES
OF BORDEAUX

THE
RED WINES
OF BORDEAUX

WILLIAM BOLTER

Series Editor: Simon Loftus

OCTOPUS BOOKS

Half title page picture
Harvesting the grapes in Latour fields, one of
Bordeaux's first growths.

Title page picture
Rows of well-tended vines in the vineyards of
St Emilion.

First published 1988
by Octopus Books Limited
Michelin House
81 Fulham Road
London SW3 6RB

ISBN 0 7064 3197 9

Printed by Mandarin Offset in Hong Kong

CONTENTS

FOREWORD

The first wine that I remember tasting was a great claret. I was seven years old when the February floods of 1953 devastated the East Coast of England and left our Suffolk farmhouse marooned in an apparently endless expanse of water – which also filled up the cellar, drowning my father's small and rather odd assortment of wines. Before the labels soaked off in the floods, these could have been identified as ranging from cheap Algerian red to 1945 Château Mouton Rothschild, Année de la Victoire. Afterwards, when the fire brigade had pumped out the cellar, it was a matter of guesswork, aided by the decipherment of embossed capsule or branded cork. Fearful of the effect of salt water on fine wine, my father decided to sample his stock, and I was allowed to sniff and to sip just a little.

Two tastes stick in the mind. One was decidedly unpleasant, a bad bottle from a well-known château which has never, in subsequent years, given me any pleasure. The other was curious, a taste that at first also seemed unattractive – harsh, tough, rather dank – but which stayed in the mouth, changing, interesting, memorable and inexplicably exciting. It was the '45 Mouton, drunk years before its maturity but already showing (even to a seven-year-old boy) the promise that eventually developed into one of the most wonderful clarets of this century.

Although I could scarcely have realized it at the time, this was a classic example of the quite particular virtues which distinguish the finest red Bordeaux from the other great wines of the world: a tough, tannic structure, intriguing bouquet, considerable length and depth of flavour.

It is worth elaborating on these characteristics. The tannin is infused from the skins of the grapes during fermentation and it so happens that the varieties planted in Bordeaux (particularly Cabernet Sauvignon) are unusually rich in this initially unappetising component. It is an important structural element in wines which are made to last and evolve in bottle, astringent at first and gradually softening with age. Such ageing is expected from all the best claret and even quite modest wines from Bordeaux will improve if kept. Most other viticultural regions of the world base their winemaking on a simpler set of ambitions, producing wine for immediate consumption.

It is bottle-age which develops bouquet, that 'bunch of scents' which encourages you to stick your nose in the glass and have an uninhibited sniff. Alluring but elusive, suggesting the character of fruits or spices, or the gamey aromas of autumn, the bouquet announces the taste itself. This is likely, for Bordeaux, to be complex rather than simple in its combination of flavours, balancing length (persistence on the palate, lingering after the wine is swallowed) with considerable depth – a generosity which cannot be completely described because the impression evolves from moment to moment.

Above all, the red wines of Bordeaux can only properly be appreciated with a meal. They need food to soften the hard edges, to balance the astringency of tannin and acidity, to allow the full splendour of mature aromas and tastes to blossom in the mouth. Something quite simple will suffice, a plate of cold beef and a baked potato, but the company of friends is essential. Even modest Bordeaux demands comment, while great claret should be discussed, argued about and mulled over with like-minded enthusiasts. Don't be in a hurry — such wine, like this book, needs to be savoured.

That sounds like a rarified pleasure, accessible only to millionaires who can pay the elevated price of the finest wines. But the great strength of Bordeaux is its incredible range, the sheer quantity of good and interesting wines at all levels, from the modest family farm to the great château. That word, château, is itself remarkably elastic in its meaning, appearing on the labels of perhaps two thousand properties which sell their own wine. Although implying a great country house, it may actually signify a tumbledown barn.

Learning about the complexities of this classic region is a continuing process, because Bordeaux is changing. Ancient reputation does not always match current reality: famous properties decline through mismanagement or family feuds, while the renown of others continues to grow, thanks to wise investment and brilliant winemaking. The last quarter-century has also been a time of great technical progress and of evolving taste, resulting in better control of vinification and the desire to make wines which can be enjoyed younger than in the past. Most of these changes are apparent to the professional on the spot long before the wine writers or consumers become aware of them.

Hence the value of William Bolter's new guide. An Englishman, living and working in Bordeaux for nearly twenty years, he has the insider's understanding of his métier but the outsider's ability to stand back, to observe and to comment with objectivity on what he sees. This sense of detachment is combined with authority and an ironic wit which enlivens this highly personal, up-to-date survey of Bordeaux. He is discreet but unambiguous in his judgements, enthusiastically expert.

Which is exactly the point of this new series of wine guides. The aim is not to provide merely general information, nor to burden the reader with elaborate tasting notes on ancient vintages. On the contrary, each book combines an explanation of the geography and winemaking of the region with a tour through the vineyards that is packed with useful, specific advice for the consumer. The aim is to be of practical help, both to the tourist and the wine drinker.

Armed with this guide, you can experiment with confidence. When you pull the cork of your latest discovery it should be with pleasurable anticipation of all that is bottled up in a single magic word — Bordeaux.

SIMON LOFTUS 1988

BORDEAUX
AND ITS
RED WINES

In 1855 the famous classification of Bordeaux wines ignored St Emilion and Pomerol. Such an omission would not be made today, for both these appellations, on the right bank of the Dordogne river, are as esteemed as any other.

INTRODUCTION

The region which produces the greatest red wines in the world must have some special magic. For me, the magic of Bordeaux is expressed by the people who make the wine and trade in it. They are at once far-sighted and parochial, wildly generous and embarrassingly mean, and always preposterous as only the self-centred can be.

This curious and fascinating mixture of characteristics seems to be acquired rather than inherited, and men who have spent a full life elsewhere are overtaken by the symptoms after only a few years in Bordeaux. There was a quintessential Englishman who came to look after a very fine and famous château, one that was a household name in the circles of the rich, a cellar deity for wine-lovers. One day he is said to have spent an hour without lunch, waiting for the shops to open, because the modest *prix fixe* restaurant where he normally ate with his wife was closed. It never occurred to him to be so self-indulgent as to go down the road to another restaurant and spend the equivalent of half the price of a bottle of his wine on a better meal.

The same gentleman invested millions of pounds in winemaking equipment, and would willingly have invested more, had it been possible to persuade him that the expenditure would have increased the quality of his wine or its reputation.

This concern for reputation (which seldom degenerates into hypocrisy) is another feature of the Bordeaux mentality which has done much for wine-drinkers. That the quality of all Bordeaux wines has increased so considerably in the last 30 years is because men have wanted to improve the reputation of their wine and, at the same time, their name.

Visitors to Bordeaux often fail to realize that the world of wine centred around the city has undergone a series of changes in the past generation as great as those which have affected, for example, the aircraft industry or the hotel trade. A visitor who is shown over a wine property and taken into the *chais* (buildings above ground where wine is made and stored because the land lies so low that underground cellars would be flooded) hopes to find an age-old practice taking place in an unchanging way. His guide, whether he is aware of the visitor's expectations or not, does not mention the great changes in grape-

growing and winemaking of the last 25 years. He will explain how the barrels are still made as they were thousands of years ago, with the same clumsy sort of tools, rather than describe how something far more essential to everyone's enjoyment of wine, the 'malolactic fermentation' (see p. 22), has been understood and taken account of only since the mid-1950s. What visitor for whom wine is the stuff of dreams wishes to know such prosaic facts?

The revolution in the vineyards has been as dramatic as the revolution in the *chais*. The man who ran the farm side of a big property used to be a respected figure, with a number of men working under him, but his knowledge was generally acquired from his father and included a number of old saws, many to do with the significance of the moon. Such ways of thinking have been swept away by a new and well-educated generation of viticultural scientists who know not only what to do but why they are doing it. They have fewer workmen but more tractors, and they inspect the property they run with the confidence of the captain of a frigate.

Not all has changed, for there are unpredictable elements which human endeavour cannot control. Winemaker and merchant alike are dependant not only on hard work for the success of their enterprise, but also on the weather and the state of the market. There are years when good rather than sound wines cannot be made, and there are years when excellent wines are available at an attractive price and cannot find a buyer. Experienced members of the wine trade know how dramatic are the changes in runs of quality or good economic health. They seldom spend a period of 12 consecutive months without something to worry them, whether it is the danger of frost or the heavy stock which no one wants. Great wines are produced here but men and women are preoccupied with the same problems which faced both grower and merchants in the eighteenth century. It is one of the things which make the place and its famous produce irresistible.

The greatest of these renowned red wines (the product of great care and much human effort) are inevitably expensive: what traditional wine merchants describe as 'best' rather than everyday drinking, rare treats rather than habitual pleasures. But Bordeaux deserves its fame as much for the rich diversity of what it has to offer as for the exceptional quality of its finest châteaux. There are thousands of properties, dozens of appellations, and the thrill which even the most modest appellation can offer is enormous. Such wines have the added advantage to the consumer of being available in quantity, often at very modest prices. This book tells you something of the background of the wines from Bordeaux and their range of characteristics, but the object is to encourage you to taste them rather than just to drink them. It is not a painful task.

WINE AND FOOD IN BORDEAUX

Making great wine obviously has a great deal, perhaps everything, to do with taste. One might reasonably expect the Bordeaux area to have a large number of excellent restaurants and a local tradition of superb eating, or even something so distinguished as to be called a local gastronomy. This is not the case. There are some very fine restaurants in the Gironde department, and one is never further than 25 km/15 miles from a sound restaurant, but it is not possible to go into an unknown restaurant and be sure of getting an excellent meal. Good food in Bordeaux is more likely to be in the general French tradition than in a particular regional style.

The gastronomic specialities of the department are local products rather than the inventions of local chefs. Oysters, for example, are a minor industry of the bay of Arcachon. They are best eaten on the spot, in the summer or autumn (since the oysters have not had to be transported inland, it does not matter whether there is an 'r' in the month). Enjoy them with well-chilled, everyday wine. These are not the elegant flat oysters of Brittany, but a more basic product, and would mask the taste of the subtler dry wines.

Another speciality is shad, the big fish which is taken from the Gironde and Garonne in the spring and which distinguishes real fish-lovers from the rest. *Foie gras* (whether served in large portions by expensive restaurants or by hosts whose wives have learned from their mothers how to prepare the raw liver) is delicious, but not particularly regional. Restaurants which are trying to keep the price of gastronomy within the reach of their customers' pockets use it in wafer-thin slices to enliven salads.

A highly recommended local speciality is Pauillac lamb, which is being encouraged back into production after having become an endangered species. This very fine lamb, eaten at two months old, can now be found in a few restaurants. It is so called because the ewes come from the moors to Pauillac after the harvest and the lambs are born there in December. This is not 'salt meadow' lamb (*agneau de pré salé*), fattened in meadows which are irrigated by salt water, but an altogether finer delicacy.

Bordeaux's two real gifts to gastronomy are *Entrecôte bordelaise*, beefsteak with a vigorous sauce, and *cèpes*, big *Boletus* mushrooms which appear at the moment when the countryside around Bordeaux is at its most mysterious, in the autumn fogs. Fried in hot oil with garlic and parsley, they are delicious. The ideal conditions for the mysterious fungus *Botrytis cinerea* (essential to the great sweet wines of Sauternes) are the same as those which encourage the proliferation of *cèpes*. So in a year when generous helpings of the fresh edible mushroom abound, make a note to buy the Sauternes of that vintage.

ENTRECÔTE BORDELAISE

The entrecôte is a rib steak of clearly marbled meat with plenty of flavour, but the trencherman needs a sharp knife if he is to cut it easily. It is not for those brought up on hamburgers.

The steak should be quite big, but not more than 2 cm/¾ inch thick, and should be marinated for half an hour or more in a vegetable oil. Each individual steak should be cooked over the dry vine shoots which have been pruned in the winter, although a household grill is satisfactory to all but the purists, who find that the extra taste given by the wood puts the steak into a different and superior class of food. When cooked on one side, the steak should be turned over and the sauce added to the cooked side.

The sauce consists of bone marrow, shallots and parsley, all chopped quite finely and mixed together with salt and pepper. The most important of the ingredients is the marrow (which should be sufficient to make enough sauce to cover the meat). How much the meat should be cooked depends on the eater.

You may, in other places, even in Bordeaux, be offered various *Entrecôtes à la bordelaise* with, among other things, red wine sauces. These have nothing to do with the real *Entrecôte bordelaise* which is described above.

THE BORDEAUX REGION

All the wines which are known as the wines of Bordeaux are grown in the Gironde department, the largest of those administrative divisions of France, the *départements*, created by Napoleon after the revolution of 1789.

The Gironde lies halfway between the equator and the North Pole, almost 800 km/500 miles directly south of London. It is therefore in the southern half of France, though not the South of France which the cinema has led us to expect; true, there is a fine stretch of beach all along the Gironde coast, but it is not populated by starlets and Rolls-Royces, there are no olive trees and the weather is as difficult to predict as in Great Yarmouth.

Climate is an important factor in making wine. Indeed, it is essential to have the 'right' weather to make great wine, to produce it at an acceptable price each year and permit the grape-grower to sleep as soundly as the butcher during the period from February to October, when the vine is in constant danger from one horror or another. The right weather, first of all, does not include disastrous frosts or hailstorms. There must be enough sunshine to encourage the colouring elements in the grape skins, and sufficient warmth to ripen the berries so that the grapes can be picked in September or October under the final requirement, a dry sky. The climate of any area also affects the style of its wines to a very pronounced extent. The wines of Bordeaux are the product of a humid, oceanic climate unlike those of the sunbaked Rhône. The oceanic nature of the Bordeaux climate is abundantly clear to the summer visitor when the huge clouds roll in from the Atlantic. Although many of the millions of tons of water they contain are lost only when they reach the mountains of the Massif Central in the middle of France, the rainfall in Bordeaux is quite high and regular, both favourable factors in the making of fine wine.

But vines cannot grow in water-laden soil; drainage is vital. The fact that the region is divided by great rivers and that streams have developed, or have been developed by man, to drain the water of the major winemaking areas, is an important contributing factor to the quality of Bordeaux wines.

The significance of the soil and disposition of the vineyards is not fully understood, even though it is on these criteria (particularly that of the soil) that the laws of *appellation contrôlée* have been based since the 1930s. What can be said is that the importance of the land in the making of great wine is not quite what it was thought to be 50 years ago, and that the study of the soil alone will not permit the quality of wine produced on it to be determined. The draining capacity of the soil is, similarly, known to be vital to quality, but it is at the moment impossible to describe what sort of drainage (if any) will allow the best wines to be made: the greatest Bordeaux wines are made in soil which permits the roots to go down 10 m/30 ft – but also in soil which becomes impermeable at less than 1 m/3 ft.

Another curiosity of the region is the extent to which different centuries have seen the preference of the consumer change quite radically from one sub-area to another. The wines of Graves were famous before those of the Médoc, while at another time the wines of Fronsac were considered superior to those from Pomerol. The desire to introduce order into a changing world has encouraged different generations to make classifications, not least that major classification which is expressed by the laws of *appellation contrôlée*. Wines and tastes change, however, and as was mentioned earlier, change is much less unwelcome in Bordeaux than is generally suspected.

Perhaps the greatest element of continuity in the history of Bordeaux and the Gironde is its pride in its role as a city and area of burghers. The histories of England and of Aquitaine, of which the Gironde is a small part, were closely linked together for 300 years, from the time that Eleanor of Aquitaine brought the region as dowry to her husband Henry II until the English army under General Talbot was finally defeated in 1453 at Castillon, but there was even during this period a very real, local, middle-class force in Bordeaux. Later, under the French kings, this middle-class power was never of great political importance, but the merchants retained economic power and the great distance of the city from Paris or Versailles enabled it to concentrate on increasing its wealth and, in the eighteenth century, on making a showpiece of the town.

Throughout the eighteenth century, Bordeaux

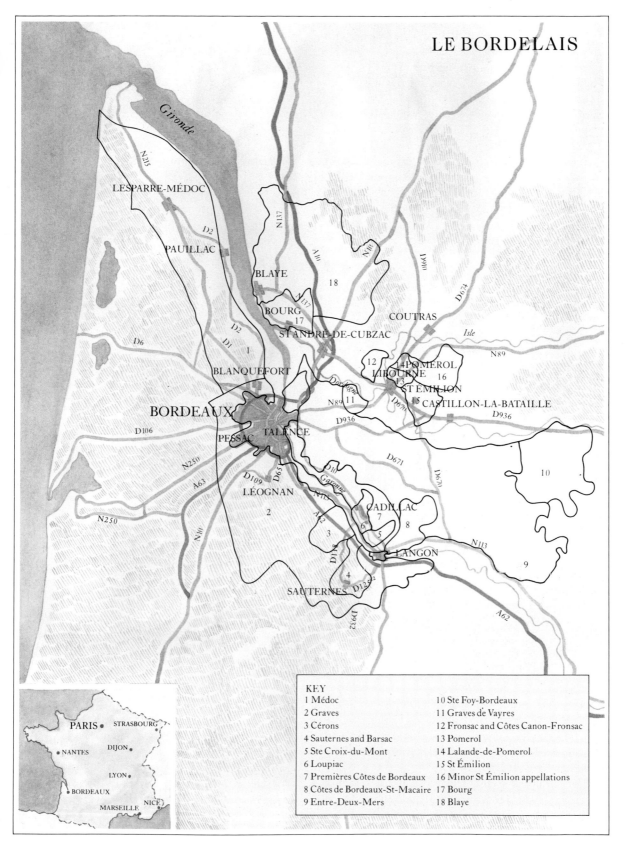

LE BORDELAIS

Gironde

LESPARRE-MÉDOC

N215

D2

PAUILLAC

BLAYE

18

D2

BOURG

D1

17

1

ST ANDRÉ-DE-CUBZAC

COUTRAS

Isle

N89

BLANQUEFORT

12

14 POMEROL

LIBOURNE

16

13

ST ÉMILION

BORDEAUX

N89

11

15

CASTILLON-LA-BATAILLE

Dordogne

D936

PESSAC

TALENCE

D936

D106

D671

D671

10

N250

LÉOGNAN

Garonne

A63

D109

D65

2

CADILLAC

N250

N10

7

8

6

5

3

LANGON

N113

4

9

SAUTERNES

D932

A62

KEY
1 Médoc   10 Ste Foy-Bordeaux
2 Graves   11 Graves de Vayres
3 Cérons   12 Fronsac and Côtes Canon-Fronsac
4 Sauternes and Barsac   13 Pomerol
5 Ste Croix-du-Mont   14 Lalande-de-Pomerol
6 Loupiac   15 St Émilion
7 Premières Côtes de Bordeaux   16 Minor St Émilion appellations
8 Côtes de Bordeaux-St-Macaire   17 Bourg
9 Entre-Deux-Mers   18 Blaye

PARIS   STRASBOURG
              DIJON
NANTES
              LYON
BORDEAUX
MARSEILLE   NICE

was the richest city in France after Paris, with its wines and its port coming right into the heart of the land without the need for artificial canals. If Montaigne is the greatest sixteenth-century writer to whom Bordeaux can lay some claim, it is the philosopher Montesquieu, a true 'bordelais' and an essentially eighteenth-century figure, who represents what the lesser aristocracy and burgher classes of the city had to offer: wit and a belief in reason.

The Continental System which Napoleon introduced at the beginning of the nineteenth century hit Bordeaux and its wine trade very hard, but the city recovered quite rapidly and demonstrated its forgiveness of the emperor by giving his name to the only bridge which crossed the Garonne river at Bordeaux. It is now known simply as the Pont de Pierre (stone bridge), and is still one of only three road bridges over the river. Bordeaux proceeded to live through the nineteenth century with a wine trade which alternately flourished and withered, but never expired. Today, the loss of the port, or at least its declining significance, has been made good by the increased production of wine and the introduction of industry (Ford has a gear-making plant and there are numerous pharmaceutical companies) to add to the city's traditional role as a regional centre.

APPELLATION CONTRÔLÉE

Wine has been made in France for centuries, time enough for the best winemaking areas to be well-known. Unfortunately, over the years a good deal of unscrupulous wine-labelling has been carried out by growers and merchants. A whole series of lawsuits in the early years of this century demonstrated the venom that this engendered. In 1935, the laws of *Appellation d'Origine* began to come into effect, and since then order has been imposed on the naming of wines to the greater benefit of the consumer and of those who draw their livelihood from wine.

The basic element in each *appellation contrôlée* is the area which it covers. Even in the smallest communes – such appellations as Pomerol – not every part is entitled to produce wine with the appellation: inspectors have charted and made known the land which is considered to be suitable for making such a wine. The criteria employed included the nature of the soil, the drainage which the plot offered, the likelihood of frost and the exposure of the land.

The commissions also decided the grape varieties which might be used, avoiding those which were over-productive or gave too coarse a taste to the wine. The method of pruning the vines was specified for each appellation, traditional methods for the production of fine wine being adopted and high-yield pruning forbidden. To make quite sure that production was kept down, limits on the total production per hectare were also laid down. The amount of sugar in the grape must (unfermented juice) was specified, since fine wine cannot be made without a sound amount of sugar coming from the grapes and being transformed into alcohol.

There is also a requirement in all the *appellation contrôlée* laws of the Bordeaux region that the final wine be submitted to a chemical analysis and a tasting by an impartial group before the *Certificat d'Agrément* is issued by the authorities and the grower has the right to sell his wine with the indication that it has the *Appellation X Contrôlée*.

These laws began to appear in the 1930s and have been revised on a number of occasions. The organization which controls the laws is the Institut National d'Appellation d'Origine des Vins et Eaux de Vie (I.N.A.O.).

There is no doubt that the task accomplished by this organization at its inception was enormous and that the laws, for which the Ministry of Agriculture is legally responsible, represent a great improvement on what existed before their promulgation.

There are, however, imperfections in the laws, partly due to the difficulty of imposing a law which affected a grower's income during a difficult time. Some of the land in the Blayais cannot have been any more suitable to the growing of wine grapes in the 1930s than it is now. Even in the most famous appellations there are plots of land which were given the right to that appellation in recompense for the fact that an inspector had, perhaps, already denied it to a high proportion of the same owner's land.

Another problem for the I.N.A.O. inspectors was and remains the withdrawal of acquired rights: it is now extremely difficult to declassify a plot of land which has proved unsuitable for wines without reimbursing the owner for his undoubted loss. The agricultural lobby in France is extremely powerful, and this may well be holding back the improvement in quality of some of the basic appellations. Another sign of conservatism on the part of the authorities is the continued existence of large parcels of grape varieties which should long ago have been grubbed up: as with many other laws, the lack of enforcement has had an unsatisfactory effect and may even have lulled the consumer into a belief that the lesser appellations have a higher guaranteed quality than is the case or it was ever the intention of the laws to ensure.

VITICULTURE –
GROWING THE GRAPES

Before planting, a grower will have the soil analysed to check, for example, its chalk content. Armed with this analysis, he will decide on the best rootstock and vine variety, probably with the help of a nurseryman.

The traditional French grape varieties can no longer be planted direct, but have to be grafted on to American root stock, which resists phylloxera, one of three terrible blights (the other two being oidium and mildew) which struck the vineyards in the nineteenth century.

Ideally, the vines are planted on land which has lain fallow for four or five years, because there are various calamities which can overtake vines planted in land which has not enjoyed this rest from viticulture. Since grapes are the only profitable crop which much of the land in the Gironde will bear, methods of ensuring that the vineyards will be safe for replanting more rapidly have of course been developed. They are not cheap.

After the vine is planted, four years go by before a crop with a right to the *appellation contrôlée* is produced, but for all that time the vine has to be tended carefully and trained along wires supported by staves. What form this wiring system takes depends on the way the vines are trained in each area, which varies quite considerably from one appellation to another.

THE YEAR IN THE VINEYARD

The first task in the winemaker's calendar is pruning, which starts in November or December, soon after everyone has recovered from the harvest and the wine has been made. How the vines are pruned depends on the traditions of each particular area. In the winter a vine grown in the Médoc looks quite unlike one grown in St Emilion. This work used to start much later, which had the advantage of reducing the risk of frost to vines which had just been pruned and were therefore most susceptible to damage. Lack of qualified workmen and the rising cost of employing them have combined to bring the date forward.

Before the first signs of life cheer the rather bleak prospect of vineyards in the winter, the first spraying of the vines (to protect against fungi) is carried out.

Further treatments against oidium and mildew are given in April, when the buds are bursting. There is now a long period until the days of the so-called Ice Saints are past and the danger of frost is over. These saints are Sts Mamertus, Pancras and Servatius on 11, 12 and 13 May respectively. The danger of frost at this late stage is still serious but the greatest damage which can be done now is the loss of a crop. The terrible frost of 1956 which killed off whole vineyards in parts of St Emilion occurred much earlier, in February, under freak conditions.

Oak vats and winemaking equipment are still widely used, as here in Pomerol, but the cost of new oak is prohibitive.

The vines flower at the beginning of June and there is another tense moment as the grower waits to see whether there is serious flower-fall. There is always some, and he cannot be sure how insignificant it is until the grapes start to swell, usually in the first week of July. Cold, wet weather at the flowering can dramatically reduce the size of the eventual crop. As soon as the flowering is over, the spraying pattern against fungal diseases and insect predators begins. This usually consists of two sprays a month, with more in hot, humid weather and fewer in dry, warm periods.

In August the grapes change colour and become (for red varieties) black rather than green. From the date of the flowering and the date of the change of colour, the grower knows when the harvest is likely to begin. The date will probably be in late September, according to the average of the last ten years, but it is extremely variable and would vary even more if the big proprietors did not have to contract for pickers as early as May or June.

Ideally, picking takes place in warm, dry weather. Hot weather means hot grapes and consequently grape juice which starts to ferment at a higher temperature than is desirable. Wet weather means an inevitable dilution of the must (grape juice). Both hot and wet weather have a reputation for begetting ill temper among the pickers, but the best properties still choose to pick by hand rather than by machine.

Machines offer advantages as well as disadvantages. If rain threatens, it is possible to pick through the night and bring in a crop of dry grapes and for economic reasons alone the machine will no doubt replace people for picking at most properties over the next ten years. At present, however, the evidence of quality as the grapes come into the vat room is still in favour of hand-picking.

Against the background of Château Latour, one of the greatest properties in the Médoc,
a modern machine is at work, spraying against the several fungus parasites which
attack the vine.

The picker empties her basket of grapes into an hotte, *the funnel-shaped container the young man carries on his back. He, in turn, will tip his load into a skip waiting at the end of the row.*

The weather during the harvest is of enormous importance for the quality of the wine produced, though its significance is declining as ways of combating rot are developed. There has not been a dangerous amount of rot at a harvest since 1968, and it may be that this is at least one of the dangers which kept nervous growers awake ten or twenty years ago that no longer has to be reckoned with.

THE VINTAGE

That the grape-grower is less at the mercy of the elements than once he was does not mean that the vintage on a bottle has lost its meaning; it does mean that what you find inside is less likely to be disappointing. The importance of the vintage, as distinct from the name of the property, is in indicating whether a wine is likely to be light or richly concentrated; whether it is ready to drink, past its best or some way from maturity. The characteristics of the vintage are very intimately connected with the weather of the year in question, but the position is somewhat complicated by the existence of micro-climates within the Bordeaux region. In 1979 the wines from the right bank of the Dordogne (St Emilion and Pomerol) were better than those from the left bank of the Gironde (Médoc) because the weather pattern suited the grape varieties of one better than the varieties of the other area. In 1986, the reverse was the case in terms of quality, simply because the weather pattern in the Médoc peninsula was more conducive to making great wines than the quite different pattern in St Emilion.

The characteristics of each vintage for the past decade are discussed in more detail on pages 32-33.

THE GRAPE VARIETIES

In many winemaking areas, a single grape variety makes a particular wine. This makes the taster's task much easier, for while different clones of the same variety certainly give different tastes (as well as different yields), the variation in taste is slight when compared with that between separate varieties. It is much more difficult to determine the source of its characteristics when a wine is made with an arbitrary mixture of varieties.

If you are visiting a property, you should take account of the fact that when a proprietor is asked what grape varieties he has planted and in what proportion one to another, he gives the figure by hectare. This figure does not correspond to the percentage of each variety which he harvests in any year, for the varieties have wildly differing yields per hec-

tare from year to year and also because the age of a vine has an adverse effect on its production in quantity, though a favourable effect on quality. It is for this reason that plantation figures alone will not take the wine-lover very far in his attempt to discover what a claret will taste like. Fortunately for him, he will have to drink the wine itself.

Red Bordeaux wines are all made from a mixture of up to six grape varieties, which are grown on more than a dozen different rootstocks.

Cabernet Sauvignon This is the most famous of the Bordeaux grapes. It is widely grown on all the best Médoc and Graves properties, and is found in St Emilion and Pomerol . . . and Blaye and wherever else claret is made. The popularity of the variety in the finest properties is due to the distinguished and long-lasting qualities which it gives to the wine. In other parts of the Bordeaux region its popularity comes from the fact that it buds late and is more likely to avoid frost damage than, for example, the earlier-budding Merlot. Cabernet Sauvignon has a big reputation: the proprietor of a classified growth with an enviable reputation and the small grower whose wine bears a lesser appellation will both be proud to tell the visitor that they have planted this variety and less willing to mention what other grapes they have used.

Cabernet Sauvignon is usually the last variety to be picked on a property. It ripens late and does not, even when fully ripe in Bordeaux, have a high sugar content. The wine it makes has deep colour and, above all, a powerful nose which is generally described as being similar to blackcurrant, but is in fact much more complex, even when the wine is still young. It is this variety which, of the three most commonly used varieties in Bordeaux, gives most of the tannin a wine will have.

Cabernet Franc This variety is more widely planted in the St Emilion area (where it is known as Bouchet to those who plant and prune vines rather than write about them) than in the Médoc. It comes to life after the winter earlier than the Cabernet Sauvignon, but resists the rigours of frost better than another comparatively early budding variety, the Merlot. It ripens earlier than the Cabernet Sauvignon too, and makes a wine which is quite different: lighter in colour, with a nose reminiscent of cardboard (saved, in all fairness, by a hint of fragile raspberry aroma) and with a thinness which may indulgently be described as delicacy. For all these disagreeable characteristics, it is a variety which adds much when used in combination with either or both of its two chief

CABERNET SAUVIGNON   CABERNET FRANC   MERLOT

rivals in Bordeaux, Cabernet Sauvignon and Merlot. Bordeaux wines made solely from Cabernet Sauvignon or Merlot can be clumsy and unappealing. The Cabernet Franc adds what is lacking to transform the whole into good or great wine. One of the ironies of tasting is that this variety, which should add least body to a wine, is the one used in such powerful wines as Château Cheval Blanc in St Emilion, where the proportion of Cabernet Franc is two-thirds of the whole. This is only one of the many peculiarities which occur with different combinations of soil, grape variety and winemaker.

Merlot This is the variety most planted in the Gironde department and it has contributed more than any other to the improvement of the quality of basic and middle-class claret. It is the kind most popular with Bordelais pruners, for the wood is soft and much easier to cut with pruning scissors than the other varieties. It is a dangerous variety to plant in the sense that it buds early. The severe frosts of 1956 and 1984 killed more Merlot than any other variety. It is also particularly subject to flower-fall and, until 15 years ago, was often overtaken by rot. This last problem has been solved, mostly by the introduction of new rootstock but also, like the control of grey rot in general, by improved sprays. What encouraged growers to plant the variety in the face of these considerable disadvantages was its generosity in quantity and sugar in the average or good years.

The wine it produces has deep colour, much fruit, great power and enormous youthful charm. What it lacks is complexity of taste and backbone, which is why growers in the Bourgeais and elsewhere take care to have some Cabernet Sauvignon to add character and also ageing ability to their wine. In the

Médoc and the Graves, Merlot was much planted in the 1950s, but lost its popularity in the three rot-ridden vintages of 1963, 1965 and 1968. It is only now being re-introduced with any enthusiasm, and then only to an extent which will not hide the more respected personality of the Cabernet Sauvignon. In St Emilion, and perhaps even more in Pomerol, its value is fully appreciated and it is the most planted variety at almost all properties in these regions. It is the combination of a soil with a high concentration of clay just below the surface and the Merlot grape variety which gives the very finest, luscious wines that most of us identify with the best of these regions.

Côt Rarely planted now, Côt (also known as Malbec) is still quite commonly found, especially in the lesser appellations. It gives a thin wine with a pleasing, highly perfumed nose, but it is difficult to vinify and to age without blending because of its low acidity and lack of alcohol.

Petit Verdot This variety is a *cépage médecin*, a cure-all variety in the Médoc. Alone, it would produce a small quantity of deeply coloured wine with high acidity and tannin which would find few takers. When blended in quite small amounts it adds vigour and colour to the whole, and is still sought after despite the fact that it ripens late and with difficulty. Outside the Médoc its production is too small, and the qualities it offers too esoteric for it to be seen. The variety is not one of those allowed by the *appellation contrôlée* authorities to be used in the making of St Emilion or Pomerol wines.

Carmenère The laws of *appellation contrôlée* permit the use of Carmenère in the Gironde. It is not a variety that the author has encountered, although it is said to be scattered throughout the region.

VINIFICATION –
MAKING THE WINE

Making red wine in Bordeaux is a much easier task than making white, since all problems come with some warning, and red wine is much more robust than white. This does not mean that there is not at least as much variation in the quality of red wine-making as of white, but it does mean that unsound red wine must be regarded as a serious reproach to the man who made it.

When the grapes are harvested, at the end of September or in October, they are generally put into a *fouloir égrappoir*, a crusher and stemmer. This machine breaks the skins of the grapes, but does not crush what goes through very forcefully: the pips are left intact, and the stalks, which are removed in a separate operation after the crushing, are not ground so hard that their sap goes into the grape must.

What goes into the vat is the juice which has run out of the crushing, and the grape-pips, skins and pulp. The liquid of this mass is still colourless, although all the grape varieties used in the making of red Bordeaux wines, unlike some Rhône wines, for example, are black grapes: the colour is in the skins and is extracted only when fermentation starts.

The vats in which the fermentation takes place may be made of wood, cement or stainless steel. Oak vats, usually about 3 m/10 ft in height and diameter, are the traditional winemaking container and are extremely appealing to the eye. They have serious disadvantages, since wood harbours bacterial matter which is anathema to the wine chemist and any cooling has to be carried out by circulating the wine through a cooling machine rather than merely pouring cold water over the outside of the vat as can be done with the modern enclosed tanks made of stainless steel. These disadvantages have not discouraged all properties from using them and even buying new ones. The owners who do so claim that the wood, being a poor conductor of heat, allows the fermentation to take place in conditions where changes are less abrupt than in stainless steel and that the wine is better as a result. They dismiss the fact that cleaning and sterilizing the wood is a difficult task (perhaps actually impossible in scientific terms) by pointing out that the whole vinification process is one of bacterial activity and that the alcohol of the wine will protect it from any ill effects.

The vat material most commonly used in Bordeaux is cement. The interior of such vats is usually coated with tartaric acid crystals or some other protective layer to prevent damage from the interaction of the active elements in the must with the cement which could eventually lead to the wine coming into contact with the steel reinforcement. When properly coated, cement vats are easily cleaned and have the same advantage of slow heat loss as wooden vats, though to an even greater extent. For the same reason, cooling has to be carried out by circulating the grape juice through an outside cooler during fermentation. This is a slow method and one which requires a cooler, a piece of equipment which probably less than half the small growers own. In times of crisis, they simply toss in plastic bags full of ice.

Stainless steel vats became very popular some 20 years ago, when the possibility of controlling the temperature of the grape must during fermentation, both by heating the liquid and cooling it, appeared to give the winemaker a power which he had not previously enjoyed. There is no doubt that the advantages of such vats are great, but the disadvantages of extreme changes in the fermentation pattern have also made themselves felt. Unless a property is very expensively equipped, the malolactic fermentation (see p. 22) can be difficult to complete.

The grape juice ferments as a result of the action of wild yeasts which are naturally present on the skins of the grapes and also in the vat room. Some growers claim good results from cultured yeast strains, but this is a matter of debate and is not yet common practice in Bordeaux. The first vat may take some time to begin fermenting, but later vats start almost as soon as the grape juice is run into the vat. The fermentation process transforms the sugar in the grapes into alcohol and carbon dioxide gas, a process which is accompanied by an increase in temperature.

In years when the grapes have not ripened sufficiently to produce enough natural sugar, some chaptalization may be necessary. This is the legally controlled addition of refined sugar to the fermenting must, to produce a stable and well-balanced wine.

During fermentation, which generally takes from three to eight days, the solid matter comes to the top of the vat and this *chapeau* (literally 'hat') or layer floating on the wine has the juice pumped over it several times a day during fermentation. This process ensures that the sugars ferment fully out and it keeps a level of carbon dioxide on the top of the vat. Carbon dioxide is heavier than air and prevents any undesirable decomposition of the solid matter, as well as aiding the extraction of colour and tannins from the skins of the grapes.

While the fermentation is taking place, the colour from the grape skins becomes soluble and the liquid, half must and half wine, goes from white to pink to red. The tannins, all contained in the solid matter of the grapes, are also extracted. This is the ingredient that gives the wine the ability to age gracefully.

If the harvest takes place in hot weather, the grapes brought in are warm. This fact, combined with the increase in heat caused by the fermentation itself, is enough to bring the overall temperature of the fermenting wine to above 29°C/84°F. Traditional vinifiers regard this as a danger point and start cooling at a much lower level to make quite sure that it is not passed, but others argue that a higher temperature is not only safe but also desirable for the best extract of colour and aromatic compounds from the grape skins.

When all the sugar has been transformed into alcohol, the wine is usually left in its vat to macerate with the solid matter for up to ten or even 15 days. The wine is pumped into, rather than over, the solid matter once a day, so that the maceration process can be encouraged.

This last period is reduced for wines intended for early drinking, since the products of maceration are those that go with long-lasting wines and most Bordeaux wine is made for people with little patience.

The wine made as described above is the *vin de*

Before machines took over, grapes were separated from their stalks prior to being put into the vats by being rubbed over the wooden lattice-work tray shown here on its side.

This impressive row of stainless steel vinification vats is at Château d'Issan – ironically, one of the oldest buildings in the Médoc. Amongst other advantages, stainless steel vats can be cleaned more easily than wooden ones.

goutte or first wine. After it has been run off into another vat, a *vin de presse* (press wine) is made by crushing the remaining solid matter which, rather like a sponge, holds a great deal of wine. This wine has different characteristics from the first wine, its more intimate contact with the solid matter adding much more tannin and colour. All this *vin de presse* may be added to the first wine, but usually only a proportion is used, the remainder being given to the property's personnel, who are entitled to a litre per day as a perk of the job. How much of this dark, bitter press wine goes into the final blend depends on the character of the vintage: in a year without high tannin content or acidity (like 1982), but with a lot of

fruit and alcohol in the first wine, more *vin de presse* would be added than in a vintage like 1984, when the wines had less power and seemed tannic even without the addition of press wine.

When the wine has completed the fermentation of sugar into alcohol, it goes through a second fermentation in which malic acid, with its pronounced and aggressive taste, is transformed into the gentler lactic acid. This process is called malolactic fermentation. It is best carried out as soon as the wine is made, before the cold weather starts. It is because this second fermentation requires a temperature of 20°C/68°F or more to take place that vinification in materials like oak and cement, which retain the heat of the wine, have an advantage over all but the most sophisticated of the modern stainless steel vats.

After the malolactic fermentation, the wine is taken from its lees (the sediment of precipitated solids and dead yeast cells) and between that time and the March of the following year, depending on the winemaker, it is matured in vat or, at the better properties, in oak casks. These oak barrels may be new or old. For the last few years, the sale price of wine and the enthusiasm of the consumer for the hint of vanilla which new oak gives a wine have encouraged the use of new barrels (which are extremely costly), but fewer than ten properties throughout the region probably use entirely new oak for every crop. Most use between a third and a half of new casks, the remainder being barrels which have already held wine. The great majority of modest properties in the Bordeaux region age their wine in vat, not cask.

This outline of vinification is the norm, but there are of course numerous variations. One that has an appreciable effect on the taste of the wine is the use – generally by small properties – of *fouloirs* (crushers) which do not remove the stems from the grapes before the must is pumped into the vats. The result is a fermentation which is cooler than otherwise and a hint of green, of grass, in the taste which is not unpleasant, although such wines are never great.

Over the last ten years there has been a movement towards fermenting wines at up to 35°C/95°F. (Vinification above this temperature is not possible because the yeast is killed off by the heat.) Wines vinified at these higher temperatures have great smoothness, but their critics find them lacking in depth. The best known wines in question are frequently from Graves vineyards, Domaine de Chevalier and Fieuzal being two such examples.

An experiment which has been extremely successful at a handful of properties is warming the wine after the fermentation is completed to extract more from the solid matter during the maceration than at the customary lower temperatures.

Less popular nowadays is the use of carbonic maceration, a technique that was most often encountered in the Graves. The method consists of putting whole bunches of grapes, without crushing or stemming, into a vat filled with carbon dioxide gas which encourages a slow, inter-cellular fermentation with much extraction of fruit from the grape and little tannin. Perhaps the cost of this process has discouraged growers from using it as much as the result, which was to produce wines with considerable fruit and charm but a somewhat un-claret-like taste.

DECANTING

Because red Bordeaux wines spend so much time in contact with the skins and pulp of the grapes, they contain a number of trace elements which are not present to any considerable degree in any white wines. A consequence of this is that they are much more inclined to throw a sediment in bottle.

In young wines this sediment is usually of crystals of potassium bitartrate, which look rather like sugar crystals which have taken on some colour from the wine. The crystals are perfectly natural and come from the tartaric acid and potassium which is in the grapes. These sugar-like deposits appear when red wine is cooled severely, and many wines which had been bottled before the very severe winter of 1984 and kept in uninsulated cellars have them. The quality of such wines is in no way impaired and neither is the consumer's health. On the contrary, this is the sign of a natural, untreated wine. If the bottle you intend to drink contains the coarse crystals of potassium bitartrate, you need not decant it. It is sufficient to pour the wine carefully.

The deposit found in many older wines is finer and more complex but, again, quite natural. It is much more likely to make the wine cloudy as the bottle is tipped when pouring and the taste may be seriously affected. To avoid this, it is advisable to decant the wine. Ideally, the bottle in question should be left standing upright for a day or two beforehand. When the time has come to decant the wine (two hours or so before the time it is to be consumed), remove the cork as gently as possible and pour the wine into a decanter (or, equally well, an empty bottle) while inspecting the flow of wine in the neck of the bottle. A candle is the traditional light source, but any lamp which permits the clarity of the wine flowing through the neck to be seen is acceptable. As soon as there are signs that the wine contains sediment, the pouring should be stopped.

It is important not to interrupt the pouring during the process of decanting for the result is inevitably a mixing of sediment and wine which is unlikely to be good to drink.

A word of warning. The very oldest wines may be too fragile to survive for long once opened and they should only be decanted immediately before serving.

Decanting can also be carried out with younger red wines without a sediment in order to allow them to 'breathe', the word used to describe the releasing of the bouquet and taste which wines, like perfumes, need to show at their best. This is an easier process, being merely the transfer of wine from one bottle to a decanter or other bottle, which should also be done two hours or so before the wine is to be drunk.

THE PRODUCERS

At first sight, the Bordeaux wine trade of the nineteenth century looks extremely simple. Growers made wine and merchants sold it and the only other people closely involved in the trade had nothing to do with the wine, but merely with the supply of corks and barrels and other items needed in the process of winemaking or wine-merchanting. That this is a superficial view is clear from the fact that three huge catastrophes, caused by the failure of the grape growers to combat the hazards of mildew, oidium and phylloxera, must have encouraged the influx of outside capital and direct selling on the part of the owners of major properties.

Nonetheless, the market was basically simpler before the worldwide economic crash of the 1930s. The merchant (*négociant*) was indispensable, not only because he knew better than the grower how to distribute wine, but because in a period when less was known of wine's chemistry, it was thought necessary to keep it in barrel much longer. Financing this ageing of the wine called for a rich merchant in addition to a well-financed winemaker.

The grower's task, too, was simpler than today in that the merchant bought his wine in cask shortly after the harvest and supervised its maturation in his own cellars in Bordeaux. This work of *élevage* (nursing the wine during its time in cask) required experience and skill. The *négociant* further justified his position by his talent for blending what would now be the lesser appellations to make a regular brand, sold as a *monopole*, which was the merchant's basic commodity. The export buyer and the consumer rarely knew where their claret came from and even the grandest wines like the first-growths from the Médoc were bottled by merchants at widely differing times.

The way the market was organized changed very greatly in the 1930s. The main reason was, of course, the economic crisis which overtook the whole of Europe, but it was exacerbated by a series of poor vintages which make the 1930s the saddest decade for clarets this century. The merchants were unable to buy wines because of lack of capital, and the smaller growers were placed in an impossible situation.

One reaction to the dilemma was the formation of the *caves coopératives*. Throughout the Gironde, the growers (mostly, but not always, from small properties) banded together to build establishments for making and storing wine. They were able to obtain help from the government in this enterprise. The disasters of this epoch also encouraged the movement towards the legal definition of the better wine-producing areas which resulted in the laws of *appellation contrôlée*, a fine example of good coming out of adversity.

The full effect of these two measures, and of many other small changes, became evident after the Second World War. The commanding position of the merchants was challenged by growers who felt that the difficulties they had known in the 1930s should not be allowed to happen again. Since then, there has been an enormous improvement in the range and quality of products available to the grape grower to arm himself against damage from all the problems which vines are heir to. Furthermore, botanical research has made possible clonal selection of vines, which has nearly always had an improving effect on the quality and quantity of wine produced each year.

Research has also enabled wine chemists to understand processes which could not previously be controlled. Wine can now be bottled earlier than before without loss of quality, because the bottled wine can be guaranteed free of flaws.

The combined effects of these changes have been to encourage château-bottling by the winemaker and to bring the consumer or export buyer closer to the growers than before. Although the merchant retains his position as the salesman of the trade, his name is less known than it was and his *monopole* usually has a dwindling importance both in the eyes of his buyer and his accountant.

The *caves coopératives* have now existed for up to 50 years, and have taken on individual personalities. They produce about a quarter of the red wine of Bordeaux in any harvest, the best less good, the worst less poor than the wines made by individual growers. Many of the *caves* now by-pass the traditional merchants in the selling of their wine and this is also true of the individual growers, who have been astute in establishing a sufficiently large private clientele to obtain independence from the merchants while taking advantage of them for export sales.

Madame Marguerite Cruse (above left) examines the colour of the wine she has made at Château d'Issan in the traditional fashion of the Bordeaux wine trade. Baron Philippe de Rothschild (above right) is shown against the vines of Château Mouton Rothschild. Both became great figures in the wine world.

The market continues to evolve quite rapidly and it will no doubt become more diverse with time. It is already clear that the huge investments made by financial institutions in the purchase of major châteaux can only be justified by an increase in the price of such wines. This may put the merchant in the position of a broker, negotiating sales from the producer for a modest commission, rather than a stock-holder taking a larger share of the profits. On the other hand, the big harvests which Bordeaux has been experiencing present the small growers with a selling task which only the *négociant*, specialized in this field, can perform.

The very number of growths (there are more than 3,000 individual properties in the Gironde depart-ment, many of them quite sizeable compared with other French vineyards) and the very small number known to anyone outside the trade encourage the thought that the growers (who complain of the mer-chants' lack of sympathy when the less attractive vintages have to be sold) and the merchants (who complain of the growers' exaggerated ideas of price) will continue to squabble among themselves, com-plicating the task of the men who act as go-betweens, the brokers (known as *courtiers*). For the consumer, the effort in improving quality which is one sure result of the growers' loss of anonymity is an excel-lent thing. Whether it is the growers or the mer-chants who take most of the profit made on a wine, the man who opens the bottle is going to gain.

GRAND VIN DE BORDEAUX

CHATEAU L'EPERON

BORDEAUX

APPELLATION BORDEAUX CONTROLÉE

1982   750 ml

Sté CIVILE CHATEAU L'EPERON - PROPRIETAIRE A VERAC-Gde

MIS EN BOUTEILLE AU CHATEAU

MIS EN BOUTEILLES AU CHATEAU

CHATEAU D'AGASSAC

LUDON MÉDOC
Appellation Haut-Médoc Controlée

Société Civile, Propriétaire   Récolte 1964

PRODUCE OF FRANCE

CHÂTEAU ROUET

FRONSAC

APPELLATION FRONSAC CONTROLÉE

75cl

ROGER DANGLADE
PROPRIÉTAIRE A St-GERMAIN-LA-RIVIÈRE (GIRONDE)

Alc. 12% vol

APPELLATION MARGAUX CONTROLÉE

1962

CHÂTEAU LA TOUR DE MONS

GRAND VIN

MARGAUX

Héritiers Pierre J. DUBOS, Propriétaires   Soussans-en-Médoc

CHÂTEAU
LA TOUR HAUT BRION

GRAVES

APPELLATION GRAVES CONTRÔLÉE

Cru classé

1980

SOCIÉTÉ CIVILE DES DOMAINES WOLTNER
PROPRIÉTAIRE A TALENCE (GIRONDE) FRANCE
PRODUCE OF FRANCE
MIS EN BOUTEILLES AU CHATEAU   750 ML

A BUYER'S GUIDE

Almost all the wines from the Bordeaux region with the right to an appellation contrôlée of Bordeaux or better use the title 'château' in their name.

CHATEAU
GRAND MAYNE

1984

SAINT~ÉMILION

GRAND CRU CLASSÉ

APPELLATION St-ÉMILION GRAND CRU CONTROLÉE

Jean-Pierre Nony, Propriétaire à St Émilion (Gde)

12,5% Vol.   **MISE AU CHATEAU**   75cl

PRODUIT DE FRANCE   PRODUCE OF FRANCE

BUYING WINE

There are a great many systems of wine distribution in Great Britain, but the most obvious, the wine merchant who ventures beyond the sale of alcoholic beverages only to a small degree, is not the biggest; supermarkets sell far more wine than the rest of the retail outlets put together.

Supermarkets have an extremely high level of quality control in their wine departments and also offer a valuable and surreptitious service to the buyer by often having a back label on each bottle with information about the wine. One less attractive feature of buying wines in supermarkets (also en-countered in other outlets) is that many of the wines are sold in 70 centilitre rather than 75 centilitre bottles; the consumer gets a glass of wine less than he thought he paid for. The main problem with most British supermarkets, from the wine-buyer's point of view, is that there is rarely a wide choice, and even more rarely any range of single-vineyard wines from a major appellation.

Supermarkets in France, on the other hand, carry a large range of claret and offer the grandest names in Bordeaux as well as more modest wines for every-day drinking. Unfortunately for the consumer, the

UNDERSTANDING THE LABEL

The label is the wine's passport, proof of identity but no guarantee that the bearer is an honourable citizen. Like all such documents, it is a compro-mise between the individual's view of himself and the requirements of bureaucracy.

1 Almost all wines from the Bordeaux region with the right to an *appellation contrôlée* of Bor-deaux (or better as here) use the title 'château' in their name. This does not mean that there is a châ-teau, although there is a very handsome one at Grand Mayne (see p. 63). It does mean that there is a winemaking establishment, which may be as rudimentary as a small vat room with a crusher and stemmer and a vat. Only one château name can be used for one property's wine.

2 This is the vintage in which grapes were picked and the wine made. All the wine in the bottle must come from that vintage.

3 Any reference to a wine being *'classé'*, whether in the Graves, the Médoc or St Emilion, must be to an official classification. For the wines of St Emilion, the classification is that of 1955, revised in 1969 and 1986.

4 The name of the district to which the *appella-tion contrôlée* refers must appear on each label, sandwiched between the words *'appellation'* and *'contrôlée'*, in the same type face and size as the appellation itself.

There are two St Emilion *appellations contrôlées* in addition to the St Emilion Grand Cru Classé classification mentioned in 3 above, St Emilion and St Emilion Grand Cru. A St Emilion Grand Cru qualifies for the more resounding title by satisfying the *appellation contrôlée* inspectors on a number of minimum requirements such as alco-holic degree and lower production which tend to ensure that the wine is better than the basic St Emilion appellation. The major hurdle for a wine which wants to qualify as being a better, Grand Cru St Emilion is in the tasting, when it will be set against other wines claiming the higher appella-tion. All wines which wish to have an *appellation contrôlée*, however grand or modest, have to sub-mit their wine to a tasting by experts, the same being taken at random by an inspector of the I.N.A.O.

5 The name and address of the producer, whether an individual or a company, must appear on each bottle.

6 The contents are sometimes expressed in milli-litres rather than centilitres, as here. The indica-tion would then be 750 ml.

advice available is not usually very informed.

Supermarkets are inclined to ignore the wine's vintage and to concentrate on the château's name, but there is really nothing wrong in that. Prices are frequently low, but you are unlikely to find the great vintages of the famous properties here. At Christmas, however, you are likely to be tempted by an exceptionally large range of wines from excellent vineyards, selling at very good prices to attract customers.

One complaint which may fairly be made about both supermarkets and the chain wine-merchant companies is that the quality control, though stringent, has a negative rather than a positive effect; the quality of the wine is sound, but not adventurous. There are, however, encouraging signs that some supermarket chains are beginning to respond to the requirements of a more discriminating clientele. The specialist wine-merchants with a store on the high street vary from relatively small divisions of vast international organizations to independent companies devoted exclusively to the buying and selling of wine. One admirable quality which they share is that of trying to inform the public. Although some of their efforts to popularize the understanding of wine may seem simplistic, there is a great deal to be learned from the information that is displayed in shops. More detailed knowledge can be gleaned from the price lists of the best merchants, who go to great lengths to put together something more than a mere catalogue of wines with prices.

Labels, leaflets, price lists: well-intentioned as they are, there is no escaping the fact that wines are to be tasted rather than written or read about, and com-

---

7 The indication that the wine is the 'produce of France' must appear on bottles destined for export markets.

8 This is a reference to alcoholic strength. It is not strictly necessary for wines sold in the United Kingdom.

9 This means that the wine was bottled on the property where it was made, by the owner. *Mise* *en bouteille du château* or *mise du château* have exactly the same meaning. The indication *mise en bouteille à la propriété* means that the wine has been produced and bottled by a *cave coopérative*.

The words *mis en bouteilles dans nos caves* mean that the wine was bottled by the name of the person or company indicated on the label and is unlikely to be the grower's bottling, but is typically a merchant's. The same holds true for the expression *mise en bouteilles dans la région de production*.

1 ——————————— CHATEAU
GRAND MAYNE
2 ———————————— 1984
SAINT~ÉMILION
GRAND CRU CLASSÉ ————————— 3
4 ————————— APPELLATION St-ÉMILION GRAND CRU CONTROLÉE
Jean-Pierre Nony, Propriétaire à St Émilion (Gde) —————— 5
8 ————— 12,5% Vol. MISE AU CHATEAU 75cl ————— 6
PRODUIT DE FRANCE   PRODUCE OF FRANCE ——— 7
9 ———————————

parative tastings, where two or more wines are tasted at the same time, are what will teach the beginner most. In wine-buying terms this means that I should prefer to seek out the merchant who puts on tastings, even if he makes a charge for participation.

Wine warehouses are a fairly new development in wine buying and while they offer bargains to those who have already learned their way about the wine trade, they are less useful to those who have not already acquired a suspicion of what they do and do not like, and what offers good value for money. There may be no one to advise you, but many wine warehouses now offer a limited opportunity for you to taste before you buy. Nonetheless, the buyer has to have his wits about him to know, for example, that the half-bottles of Château X 1978 are offered at such a reasonable price because they are a bargain rather than because the owner could not afford to bottle his wine until it had been too long in vat. If you have the knowledge, wine warehouses can offer a good hour's happy browsing and some very good drinking at below-average price. They are less common in France than in Britain, but are a growth sector of the wine market.

Mail order houses abound in the wine trade and the competition has been sufficient to encourage offers at attractive prices with a rather special line in adjectives and exclamation marks. There is sometimes a requirement that a full case of each wine be taken, which may not be to the advantage of the consumer chained to a mortgage. The ready-mixed 'tasting' cases seem frequently to contain at least one wine that no one wants to sample. The best mail order merchants, however, offer a guarantee to their customers and others might do well to emulate.

Door-to-door selling is apparently responsible for an appreciable volume of sales in Great Britain. There is nothing wrong in that, but some of it is car-ried out by the aggressive salesman who regards selling as an extension of the martial arts. These are not people to do wine business with. In France, door-to-door selling exists and is just as unexciting as in Britain, but there is a tradition of salesmen visiting customers in a fairly limited area twice a year, selling five or six cases at a time. Although the advice on offer may vary in accuracy and prices may not always be reasonable, doctors frequently buy their wine in this way and the wine served at their tables is notoriously good. This method of selling is slowly dying out, however.

Many people visit wine-producing regions in France and in any of the major areas there will be signs inviting visitors to taste and buy wines direct from the property (*dégustation/vente directe*). Such visits are always worth while. Usually the interest is in the explanation of the winemaking process and in tasting the wines. Occasionally the visitor finds that the cellar is merely a storage place from which wine is sold and that the interest of the 'visit' lies in meeting the people in what is, in fact, a shop rather than learning about wine. This is unusual, however, and a visit to a vineyard or two is strongly recommended. You should expect to buy a bottle or a carton of six bottles, according to the price and you should not boast that you have obtained a bargain until you have compared the price you paid with that of the local grocer. Usually, the grower has added on a margin to cover the extra cost of having someone available to show customers round. This is also true of buying wines direct from the property for delivery to your home: the extra cost of forwarding wine in small parcels more than eats up the advantage of buying direct. There is more to life than a search for financial advantage, however, and you may very much enjoy dealing with the man who made the wine and following his product from year to year.

PRICE STRUCTURE

Claret is available throughout the world, at all prices. If you are giving a party, and wish merely to have a wine to drink rather than taste, then a basic Bordeaux or Bordeaux Supérieur, probably labelled 'Claret', is perfectly sufficient, and should cost about £3 a bottle. Drinking it will not teach you much about wine, but that is not the point of the exercise.

The lower price range of Bordeaux wines, at about £4 a bottle, gives you the opportunity of buying château-bottled wines from a specified vintage with the appellation Bordeaux or Bordeaux Supérieur, or with an appellation such as Côtes de Blaye, Côtes de Bourg and the like.

The advantage of drinking and tasting wines in this class is that they have a more distinct character than the lower-priced wines, which are inclined to lack personality. The fact that a wine is from a single vineyard and single vintage permits you to acquire some idea of what that appellation and that vintage can produce, which is what tasting, rather than drinking wines is all about.

In the middle price range, between £4 and £7 a bottle, you have more choice and more help from your own and the wine writers' experience. Within this range there are some very fine *appellations contrôlées* along with wines from properties which you are likely to read about. Any purchase should, of course, be of a château-bottled wine with its vintage announced on the label. The reason why there is a sudden jump in quality between these and the lower-priced wines is that the fixed charges on wine remain the same in both categories; a greater proportion of the price of a £6 bottle of wine than of a £3 actually represents wine. In this price band, you will probably do best to buy a wine no more than five years old until you have decided that you like some specific older vintages.

Such is the demand for excellent claret that you must expect to pay more than £7 a bottle, at the retail level, to obtain a fine claret rather than a merely good one, and the range extends extravagantly upwards. You will note on p.33 that there are bargains to be found by seeking out the 'second wines' of the most famous properties. Nonetheless it is only at well above £10 a bottle that you will encounter the first wines of these major classified growths, and the most famous names will be yours only at three, four or five times that.

This last should not depress you, for there is a world of taste experiences to be obtained without going beyond the middle range and great vintages of claret show every sign of continuing to be made: there will be lots of exciting and very famous wines for you to try when you feel that the time is ripe to award yourself a fabulous treat.

PRICE BANDS

INEXPENSIVE
Blaye
Bordeaux
Bordeaux Supérieur
Bordeaux Supérieur Côtes de Castillon
Bordeaux Supérieur Côtes des Francs
Côtes de Bourg
Premières Côtes de Blaye
Premières Côtes de Bordeaux

MIDDLE-RANGE
Canon Fronsac
Fronsac
Graves
Haut Médoc
Lalande de Pomerol
Listrac
Lussac St Emilion
Médoc
Montagne St Emilion
Moulis
Puisseguin St Emilion
St Emilion

TOP-CLASS
Margaux
Pauillac
Pomerol
St Emilion Grand Cru
St Estèphe
St Julien

VINTAGES

In Bordeaux, each year is a 'vintage' year. Almost all château-bottled clarets give the vintage in which the grapes were harvested and the wine made on the label, but this appears as a fact rather than as a sign of excellence. Other wines, like Port and Champagne, 'declare' a vintage only in exceptionally good years. It is perhaps this fact which has encouraged consumers to attach such great importance to the vintage of a wine, be it Champagne or Bordeaux.

This does not mean that the vintage of a claret is without interest: the style of the wine and, above all, its likely maturity depend on it. But the differences are less great than is generally believed by the man eagerly scanning a vintage chart which evaluates a given vintage with a rather arbitrary mark out of ten or twenty.

It is more important to have a very general idea of the characteristics of a vintage than to trust such ratings. Even then, a few lines of comment can do no more than indicate a pattern which the wine under consideration may not follow.

There are three main reasons for this: the difference in quality between one Bordeaux region and another, the variation which springs from differing methods of vinification and the less easily definable disparities in the wines of neighbouring winemakers of similar ability.

The year of 1986 is a typical one in which the quality of two areas, St Emilion and the Médoc, varied enormously, very largely for climatic reasons (see below). The result is that some wines from the Médoc, particularly the north, are great wines. The 1986 wines of St Emilion are rarely more than good. Even this statement is an oversimplification of the complex reality.

Men make wine for sale at different prices and for consumption at different times. A very grand first growth property may vinify its wine to last for 20 years and to be at its peak only after ten years' ageing. If the producer of an excellent red Bordeaux *appellation contrôlée* wine in the area between the Garonne and Dordogne rivers were to attempt the same vinification technique, his wine would lose its charm and become something harsh and unsaleable. With famous wines, the vintage tells the consumer how well developed they are likely to be. In the case of the basic Bordeaux, the vintage can be instructive in warning the prospective buyer that the wine may be too old. The advantage of having the vintage indicated in either case is clear, its relationship to a vintage chart obviously arbitrary.

Good winemakers make less good wines in some years than in others for any number of reasons and it takes professional knowledge and memory to be able to recall that Château X made a rather poor wine in 1983, good though that vintage was. Keep these reservations in mind when reading these notes.

RED BORDEAUX 1977–86

1986 was the year when the harvest began generally at the very end of September, after a long, dry summer without any excesses of cold or hot weather. The harvest was extremely large and very uneven in quality. The best wines are those from the north of the Médoc. The wines of St Emilion are distinctly less good, perhaps because of heavy late rain and the Merlot grape's over-production. The best Médoc wines appear to have great lasting qualities.

1985 was a year of high production of almost universally good claret: certainly the Libournais wines (St Emilion and Pomerol) and the left bank wines (Graves and Médoc) show equally well. The wines are fairly fast maturing and will have great charm and elegance.

1984 produced better wines in the Médoc and Graves than in the Libournais, where the lesser growths produced dull wines. The harvest was not large, but a glut of more sought-after vintages may encourage merchants to sell off even the best 1984s at low prices. If that is the case, the wines are worth buying, though not worth laying down.

1983 produced a vintage which everyone agrees is less even across the board in quality than the 1982s, but there are many who believe that this is a longer-lasting year, with greater subtlety than its immediate predecessor. The classified châteaux will require several years' ageing. The lesser wines tend to lack obvious charm. There is no doubt the wines are very good, but how good is still difficult to judge.

1982 was a year in which a good-sized harvest was brought in unusually early, the harvest starting on 17 September. The wines produced had an obvious and immediate appeal, and a concentration which ensured good lasting qualities. The best have a long life before them. It is rare to have a harvest of such ripe grapes, and the best are full-bodied and have a rich texture and exuberance unusual for Bordeaux wines.

1981 is a vintage of clarets typical of a good, not great, year. The wines have finesse and are ageing very well, but lack the full-bodied characteristics of the 1982. This is another good year for people buying major growths now, the prices being lower than those for the 1982s and 1983s. Some of the lesser properties are beginning to look rather tired and should be tasted: they may be found to have aged fast in the last 12 months.

1980 produced delightful but rather light wines which matured very soon and have now generally been drunk.

1979 was a year of high production of sound wines, much better in St Emilion and Pomerol than in the Médoc. The best are good for a few years to come, the least good are showing a coarse quality unusual in good claret.

1978 was a very fine year, harvested in October and without the concentration of a hot year but with the complexity and lasting qualities which are looked for in a great claret vintage.

1977 is the only vintage of the decade under discussion to have produced wines which are now, with few exceptions, downright poor. Any remaining should be consumed at once.

KEY BUYING MAXIMS

1 The most important maxim is to taste before you buy if you possibly can, preferably in comparison with other wines of a similar appellation and price.

2 A deposit in a bottle of claret is not a bad sign provided that the wine is clear when held up to the light. Coarse crystals (of potassium bitartrate) which lie at the bottom of the bottle almost always come from tartaric acid, which is found naturally in grapes (see p. 23).

3 The best Bordeaux wines are designed for keeping. They need some period of bottle age to express their full potential. The length of the cork is important. For modest wines (to be kept up to 18 months) 3 cm/1¼ inches will do. The classic bottles, intended to mature for up to 20 years, need a longer cork, at least 4 cm/1¾ inches.

4 Except for daily drinking, as the traditional phrase has it, go for château-bottled rather than merchant-bottled claret. Every time a wine is moved or pumped, it suffers. Better to bottle at source. This advice would have been quite different 20 or so years ago, when château-bottling at the smaller properties was frequently carried out in appalling conditions.

5 Do not buy wine which is too expensive for your pocket.

6 Do buy the occasional bottle which is hopelessly too expensive for your pocket, just to see why people get so excited about it. Such extravagances should be carefully planned, in consultation with a supplier whom you have learned to trust.

7 Most of the top properties in Bordeaux produce second wines under a different label which are made from those vats which didn't quite achieve the quality required for the first wine. Some of these offer excellent bargains for the wine-lover.

8 The advice of an honest merchant is of more use than the often outdated status implied by the official classifications.

9 Do not think that because you have tasted a wine and found it unattractive to your palate, it or you will not mellow. Taste it again if you can, and see whether one of you has changed.

10 It is always unwise to buy a wine which a friend recommends without first tasting it yourself, for his taste may be different from yours. It is always a good idea to taste with other people, since their experience may help you.

11 Never think that a wine cannot be good because it is inexpensive, although price and quality, in wine as elsewhere, are very closely related.

THROUGH
THE
VINEYARDS

*Vines are more densely planted in the Médoc than elsewhere
in the Bordeaux region, as in these vineyards in St Estèphe, one of the
communes privileged to have its own* appellation contrôlée.

Before starting on our tour of the vineyards, it may be as well to explain how the gradation of the different appellations in Bordeaux is constructed. Wine made from the permitted grape varieties on suitable land anywhere within the Gironde department may, subject to a tasting test, be entitled to the basic appellation Bordeaux. This vast region is subdivided into a number of distinctive areas (Médoc, Graves, St Emilion, etc). These areas in their turn may be further divided into specific local appellations centred on a particular town or village. In the Médoc region, to take an example, most of the best-quality wines would qualify for the designation Margaux, St Julien, Pauillac or St Estèphe.

Each of these appellations will be dealt with in its turn. However, in a wine-producing region as complex as Bordeaux, it is impossible to construct a completely logical tour, but my intention has been to move, in very general terms, from the famous grand classic regions of Bordeaux to those which produce a larger quantity of more modest wines and which, perhaps, are lesser known.

These well-tended rows of vines are in St Emilion, and give some indication of the hilly countryside which is such a refreshing aspect of the commune compared to the flat land of the Médoc and Graves.

THE MÉDOC

The Médoc is the name of the peninsula of land which extends north-west from just outside Bordeaux and which lies between the Atlantic Ocean and the Gironde estuary. It is flat and also very quiet, not on the road to any city, and anyone who is in the Médoc is generally there because he has business there or because he wishes to view the vineyards.

The boundary separating the Graves appellation, which surrounds Bordeaux, from the Médoc is a stream, the Jalle de Blanquefort, 10 km/6 miles from Bordeaux. As you drive north on a minor road, the D2, the poverty of the land and the grandeur of the estates becomes clear. The small houses nag at the edges of the villages and clutter up the countryside, but the châteaux, sometimes in very generous grounds and frequently very lovely in addition to being very grand, demonstrate that there is wealth here. Anyone who has read the wine lists of the great restaurants throughout the world will know why: the appallingly poor land produces huge quantities of the most subtle and sought-after wine made anywhere. Wines are described as fine in an off-hand manner, but the word takes on all its meaning in relation to the best wines of the Médoc: they are fine in that they are elegant, complex and restrained, a true and unusual pleasure to drink. The fact that they are generally produced by properties with large acreage means that these wines are widely distributed. They are as universal as great wines can be and, at their best, incomparable.

The D2 leaves Bordeaux via the suburb of Blanquefort, heads north through land with the right to the appellation Haut Médoc, traverses a cluster of renowned hamlets with the right to the more limited appellation of Margaux, and subsides once more into the less distinguished terrain of the Haut Médoc. Continuing north, it passes through the adjoining communes of St Julien, Pauillac and St Estèphe, after which there is another stretch of vineyards with the right to the description Haut Médoc and then an area which simply merits the basic appellation which all the wines of the peninsula can claim, Médoc. At the town of Lesparre, you can turn back south to Bordeaux on a road which lies further west, closer to the pine forests and further from the Gironde estuary. This route will take you through the other two commune appellations, Listrac and Moulis, which lie to the west of Margaux.

The wine-producing part of the Médoc is a very small strip of land, a series of gravel banks interrupted by streams and ditches and low-lying meadows, bounded on one side by the estuary and on the other by the dense pine forest which separates it from the Atlantic. The pines and the estuary are never far from sight, even in this flat land. Everything in the landscape goes to show that the Latin from which the Médoc takes it name, *in medio aquae*, was well expressed.

THE SOUTHERN MÉDOC

Château Dillon is an agricultural school as well as being a wine-producing property. It is on the far side of Blanquefort from Bordeaux, and invites visitors to come and taste an Haut Médoc which is usually extremely agreeable.

The first of the classified châteaux on this D2 road is **Château la Lagune** which, having fallen into decline in the 1950s, was completely replanted and put into order by a talented new owner who had the misfortune of harvesting a tiny crop in 1961, a year of great quality but very limited production (12 per cent of what was made in 1986). The property was sold again soon after this, but can still be counted on to produce good wine even in poor years. La Lagune is in the commune of Ludon, an area with the right to the Haut Médoc appellation. In the same commune, nearer the estuary, is a moated fourteenth-century fort, **Château d'Agassac**, which is also a regular source of sound Haut Médoc, although not a classified growth.

Continuing on the road from Blanquefort to Margaux, **Château Cantemerle** is the next major growth after la Lagune. Château Cantemerle is the last in the 1855 list of the classified growths of the Médoc and its name was added in a different hand. The reason for this is believed to be administrative forgetfulness and certainly the wine produced is excellent, traditionally delicate rather than full-bodied, with great charm. The property changed hands in 1981, and the wines have gradually begun to show more concentration.

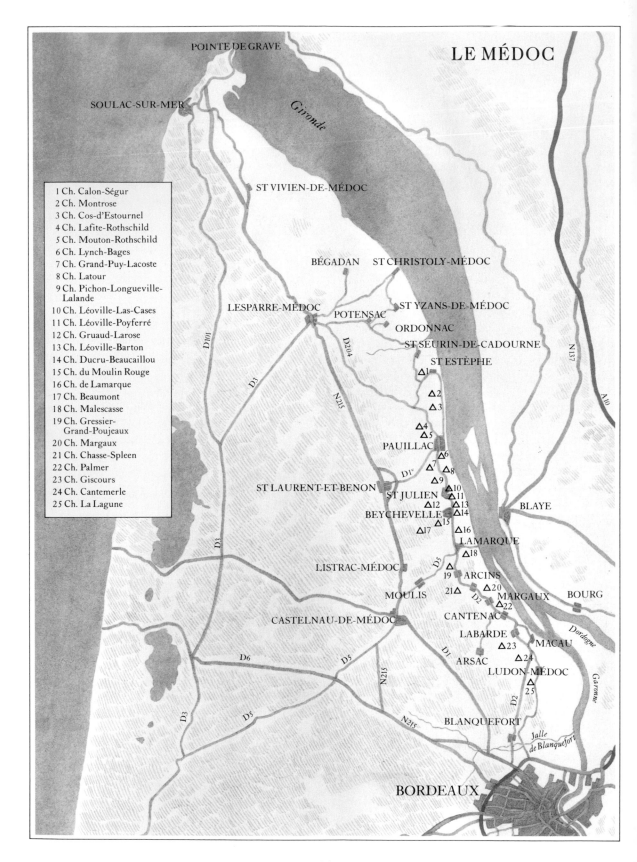

LE MÉDOC

POINTE DE GRAVE

SOULAC-SUR-MER

Gironde

ST VIVIEN-DE-MÉDOC

1 Ch. Calon-Ségur
2 Ch. Montrose
3 Ch. Cos-d'Estournel
4 Ch. Lafite-Rothschild
5 Ch. Mouton-Rothschild
6 Ch. Lynch-Bages
7 Ch. Grand-Puy-Lacoste
8 Ch. Latour
9 Ch. Pichon-Longueville-
   Lalande
10 Ch. Léoville-Las-Cases
11 Ch. Léoville-Poyferré
12 Ch. Gruaud-Larose
13 Ch. Léoville-Barton
14 Ch. Ducru-Beaucaillou
15 Ch. du Moulin Rouge
16 Ch. de Lamarque
17 Ch. Beaumont
18 Ch. Malescasse
19 Ch. Gressier-
   Grand-Poujeaux
20 Ch. Margaux
21 Ch. Chasse-Spleen
22 Ch. Palmer
23 Ch. Giscours
24 Ch. Cantemerle
25 Ch. La Lagune

BÉGADAN   ST CHRISTOLY-MÉDOC

LESPARRE-MÉDOC   POTENSAC   ST YZANS-DE-MÉDOC

ORDONNAC

ST SEURIN-DE-CADOURNE

ST ESTÈPHE

△1

△2

△3

△4
△5

PAUILLAC

△6
△7 △8
△9
△10
ST JULIEN △11
△12 △13
BEYCHEVELLE △14
△15
△17 △16

ST LAURENT-ET-BENON

LAMARQUE

△18

BLAYE

LISTRAC-MÉDOC

19△ ARCINS

21△ △20
MOULIS MARGAUX BOURG
△22

CANTENAC

CASTELNAU-DE-MÉDOC

LABARDE
△23 MACAU

△24

ARSAC LUDON-MÉDOC
△25

Dordogne

Garonne

BLANQUEFORT

Jalle de Blanquefort

BORDEAUX

MARGAUX

The *appellation contrôlée* Margaux extends to four communes in addition to Margaux itself. The first of these on the Médoc road is Labarde, which has two classified growths, **Château Giscours** and **Château Dauzac**. Château Giscours is a very large property both in acreage and buildings. The wine here is usually deep in colour and rather slow to develop into the very lovely and attractive wine it is when properly aged. This is one of the longer-lasting of the major Margaux growths. However, the obvious elegance of the best wines of this appellation should not mislead the taster into thinking that they lack staying power or quickly deteriorate.

Another growth in this commune is **Château Siran**, which has a reputation for rather lighter but also long-lasting wine.

Cantenac, the next commune whose wines enjoy the right to the appellation Margaux, has a number of classified growths: Château Brane Cantenac, Château Palmer, Château Boyd Cantenac, Château d'Issan, Château Kirwan, Château Cantenac Brown, Château Prieuré Lichine and Château Pouget.

The most famous of these is **Château Palmer**, which is particularly well situated and has been managed for many years by the Chardon family, who have established the fame of the wine as second only to the first growths. The estate is widely planted in Merlot, and there is also a significant percentage of Petit Verdot. The result is a rich wine of deep colour which is noted for succeeding well in years of lesser fame.

Château Prieuré Lichine is the estate of Alexis Lichine, one of the men who have done most for Bordeaux wines, and especially the grander appellations, since 1945. His property can be visited on any day of the year and you will be shown wines with deep colour, much fruit on the nose and palate and with fewer of the more severe qualities which are necessary if a wine is to be aged for a long time. A map of this property is extremely interesting in showing the way properties are built up by the purchase of small parcels in the commune. Such divided properties make working the land a more complicated task than on estates which consist of a large, single parcel of land, but they do have the advantage that in years of frost or hail the risk of damage to the entire crop is reduced.

The major part of **Château d'Angludet** is planted in Cabernet Sauvignon, which is the great variety in the Médoc. The property produces a wine of great

The splendid Château d'Issan, one of the oldest properties in the Médoc, is surrounded by a moat which dates from medieval times.

Château Palmer was built in the 1850s. The three flags, French, Dutch and British, which fly from the roof signal the origins of the owners, but the château is uninhabited.

distinction which is well worth looking out for. It is the home of Peter Sichel, a major shareholder in Château Palmer.

South of Cantenac is a small commune, from the viticultural point of view, part of which has the right to the appellation Margaux and which can boast one classified growth, **Château du Tertre** (*tertre* is a word for hill, and the property is on what might, just, be called a hillock). This is a property whose wines vary in quality to a marked degree, but the best of the years, such as the 1985, have proved to be excellent.

The commune of Margaux itself has the first growth **Château Margaux** within its limits. This is a classical Greek temple of a building, constructed in the first years of the nineteenth century by Combes, whose masterpiece it is. The splendour of the property is everywhere apparent, with *chais* and work-buildings conceived on a very grand scale and forming a very impressive estate.

The Mentzelopoulos family have spent a fortune on the renovation of the château, cellars and vineyards and the wine is now on a par with the property, and is one of the best in Bordeaux. No estate is consistently the best in every major vintage but Château Margaux comes as near to doing this as

can be done and has sometimes produced a series of vintages (1945-50, for example) when every one is superb. A recent series that promises to be almost as superb seems to have started in 1979. **Pavillon Rouge**, the second wine of Château Margaux, is an expensive bargain.

The commune also contains: Châteaux Rausan Ségla, Rauzan Gassies, Lascombes, Durfort-Vivens, Malescot St Exupéry, Marquis d'Alesme Becker, Ferrière, Desmirail, Marquis de Terme.

Château Malescot St Exupéry is one of the most interesting of these wines, since it is vinified to last for a long time, with no concession to impatient consumers. The result is a wine of deeper colour than most, with some of the austerity of the Pauillac wines, which need ageing to show at their best. The vintages to go for are the ones best noted for full ripeness of the grapes at picking.

Château Lascombes is the very reverse of Malescot, in that the winemakers seem intent on bringing out the more obviously attractive features of their wines from the first tastings. The wine has length on the palate, but is probably vinified in the best vintages to be drunk in six to eight years rather than decades after the harvest.

The commune includes several divisions of the

THE SOUTHERN MÉDOC INCLUDING MARGAUX	
Outstanding Properties	**Excellent Properties**
Cantemerle	Angludet*
Giscours	Bel-Air Marquis
La Lagune	d'Aligre*
Margaux	Boyd Cantenac
Palmer	D'Issan
	Labégorce-Zédé
	Lascombes
	Malescot St Exupéry
	Prieuré Lichine
	Du Tertre
*Can represent particular bargains	

old estate of L'Abbé Gorsse, of which the best is the well-managed property **Château Labégorce-Zédé** (partly in Soussans).

One of the most promising lesser-known wines of Margaux is **Château la Gurgue**, rapidly improving under the management of Mme Villars, of Château Chasse-Spleen (see p. 43).

The next commune to Margaux going northwards is Soussans, which has the right to the Margaux appellation, but does not have a classified growth. **Château la Tour de Mons** is a large property where delicate wines are made with that hint of violet on the nose which is supposed to distinguish Margaux wines. Here, again, the delicacy of the wines deceives many tasters into imagining that the wine will not last. This is not the case, but it is true that lesser vintages of this château sometimes tend to lack body.

Château Bel-Air Marquis d'Aligre is a fine property with the Margaux appellation, producing very attractive wines which have quite surprising depth for an unclassified château whose wine can never command the higher price of the major Margaux estates.

The fact that the appellation Margaux is spread, sometimes thinly, over five communes may explain a lack of unity of character in the best wines which can use the name. The excellent wine of a good-vintage Château Pouget is quite different from the excellent wine of the same vintage of another classified growth, Château Lascombes. No one would suggest that the area of the present appellation should be split into smaller appellations, but a reduction in the variety of the wines would make the experts' task

easier at a blind tasting. On the other hand, it may be the sign of a great appellation that it has such a wealth of properties, each with a quite different but equally valid claim to applause.

LISTRAC AND MOULIS

A detour to the west of Margaux, heading towards the pine forests, brings the visitor to an important stretch of vineyards which lie within the communes of Listrac and Moulis. The wines from these appellations seldom approach the finesse of those from the villages which lie closer to the Gironde estuary. But nonetheless both appellations have their own sturdy character which merits attention and both have increasingly become appreciated.

Like its grander neighbours to the east, Listrac is one of the individual commune appellations of the Médoc, stretching east and west across the N215. Much of its wine goes to the big *cave coopérative* in the town of Listrac and from there it is sold to the French railways, which have offered it as their staple Médoc wine for as long as anyone cares to remember. There are some excellent Listrac wines from individual properties, however, and **Château Fourcas Dupré** is one which is generally available because of the size of the property. The wine is well vinified, and has the depth of the best Médoc wines with a hint of toughness and slight lack of length of flavour which is characteristic of the Listrac appellation by comparison with the other commune appellations of the Médoc.

Another property of the commune, which defies analysis as a Listrac while undoubtedly being one, is **Château Clarke**. This estate was bought by a member of the Rothschild family in 1973, and a planting and replanting programme was undertaken on a scale worthy of the family's name. No expense was spared on the winemaking and storage facilities either, and the property is producing wines on which

LISTRAC AND MOULIS	
Outstanding Properties	**Leading Properties**
Chasse-Spleen	Clarke
Dutruch Grand Poujeaux*	Fonréaud
Gressier Grand Poujeaux*	Fourcas Dupré
Poujeaux*	Fourcas Hosten
*Can represent particular bargains	

*Château Margaux is the most impressive architectural sight
in the Médoc, now restored to its pristine glory by lavish cleaning of
the stone. The winemaking and storing buildings are just
as spectacular.*

as much expenditure in financial and human terms is being made as at many of the famous classified growths. The result is an exciting but somewhat surprising wine, with some of the finer qualities of claret clearly present but an underlying modesty of soil that inevitably shows through and can be sensed from time to time.

Just south of Listrac is the commune of Moulis, which also stretches east-west across the main road. The best property in this commune is undoubtedly **Château Chasse-Spleen**, where wine of great character has been made for the last 15 years or more. Under the enthusiastic management of Bernadette Villars, this is one of the best-run estates of the Médoc. The wine has a strong undertone of tannin, which encourages faith in its ageing ability, but is delightfully well-rounded and generous on the palate.

Another, smaller and more modestly priced property in the commune, **Château Gressier Grand Poujeaux**, is run in the traditional way, resulting in a wine with less finesse than Chasse-Spleen, but with an attractive vigour.

THE MÉDOC BETWEEN MARGAUX AND ST JULIEN

In the estuary opposite Margaux are the islands of Margaux and Cazeau, both made up largely of alluvial soil like the low-lying land at the side of the Gironde estuary. These islands and land produce some unexceptional wine, which merits no more than Bordeaux *appellation contrôlée*.

On the road from Margaux to St Julien-Beychevelle, there is a section of land with the right to Haut Médoc as an appellation, but no more. This is because the wines made here do not, traditionally, come up to the high standard of, for example, those of the commune of St Julien. The subsoil is heavier and the roots do not extend as far down as they do in the major commune appellations, where the soil allows the roots to penetrate at least 2.5 m/8 ft, sometimes deeper still. The restaurant in Arcins, the Lion d'Or, is run by a jovial gentleman who encourages customers to bring a bottle of their own wine to drink with lunch or dinner.

Just off the main road, in the village of Lamarque, are the properties of **Château de Lamarque** and **Château Malescasse**. The first of these two properties is a fourteenth-century moated fortress, run with great energy and brio, making wines which have steadily improved over the last ten years and which

must certainly be numbered among the most attractive of the appellation. Château Malescasse produces a large quantity of wine, well-made and with the distinction which Cabernet Sauvignon gives in the Médoc.

Back on the D2 road, there is the commune of Cussac Fort Médoc. The fort in question is one built by Vauban, the great French seventeenth-century military architect. This edifice, together with the grander fortress on the other side of the river in Blaye and another smaller fort on an island in the middle, was designed to guard Bordeaux from seaborne attack. This commune has some excellent 'Bourgeois Growths', the properties not classified in 1855 but whose owners qualify for this lesser title by reason of classifications carried out in 1932, 1966 and 1978. **Château Beaumont** is one of these, and is a very big and successful property run by a dynamic team. It is now owned by a financial institution, one of the first of a series of purchases by such organizations of large properties in the Médoc. The full-flavoured wine of Château Beaumont is made with excellent equipment and care, and the property is recognized to be one of the rising stars of the Haut Médoc appellation.

Château du Moulin Rouge is a family property in Cussac where three generations of the same family are now at work and where the profits are put back into the estate for the purchase of more land and the improvement and care of cellars and equipment. The wine is excellent, full-bodied and with the capacity to last well.

Just before Cussac gives way to St Julien, there is a fine château, **Lanessan**, which makes sufficient wine to have an international reputation. It always makes sound wine, and the best years have great distinction as well.

The boundary between Cussac and St Julien is, as is often the case with wine-producing boundaries, a stream. The bridge which crosses this stream is known to the inhabitants of Cussac as the 'bridge of miracles', for the wines of St Julien sell for a much higher price than those of Cussac.

BETWEEN MARGAUX AND ST JULIEN	
Excellent Properties	**Leading Properties**
Beaumont Lamarque Malescasse Moulin Rouge	Arnauld Lanessan

ST JULIEN

St Julien is a commune devoted almost entirely to wine, and one of the great debates at Bordeaux dinner tables is which of the major châteaux would be a first growth if a new classification were made today. The 'which' of the question is in the plural in everyone's mind, for there are excellent châteaux everywhere in the commune, which – unlike Margaux – does not share its appellation with any other village.

As a building, the grandest château in St Julien and one of the great architectural delights of the Médoc is undoubtedly **Beychevelle**, which also has a fine park and a commanding view over the meadows which go down to the Gironde. This is a large property which makes fine wines, but it is its neighbour, **Château Ducru Beaucaillou**, which has at the moment the enviable reputation of more regularly making great wines. It is one of the few great properties in the Médoc to be occupied by its owner, the widely respected Jean-Eugène Borie. M. Borie also makes a more modestly priced wine of excellent

quality, **Château Lalande Borie**, from a vineyard that used to form part of Château Lagrange.

The great rival to Château Ducru Beaucaillou in reputation, a trifling matter were it not for the price which reputation brings, is **Château Léoville Las Cases**, nearer Pauillac. Both the wines are made by men who have devoted their lives to their profession, and who learned how best their land would produce during the long period in the 1940s and 1950s when even classified growth wines sold for low prices. Both have perfected their art and few tasters would be presumptuous enough to make any judgement on which is the finer winemaker. Ducru is wonderfully elegant, but Léoville Las Cases tends to have greater concentration. Its second wine, **Clos du Marquis**, is excellent.

Another property with superb land which has been making excellent wine for some years is **Château Gruaud Larose**, which, with **Léoville Barton**, yet another classified growth of the commune, will run the established masters hard over the next few decades. Léoville Barton, in particular, has set a fine example for moderate prices. The third Léo-

The eighteenth-century Château Beychevelle, situated on the main road through the commune of St Julien Beychevelle, is maintained impeccably.

ville, **Léoville Poyferré**, has been making excellent, elegant wines in recent vintages.

Two other properties which have a great interest as exponents of change in what is reputed to be the settled world of wine are **Château Lagrange**, a classified growth which lies to the west of the village of St Julien, although remaining within the commune's limits, and **Château St Pierre**.

The first of these was bought in 1983 by a Japanese company, Suntory, and tremendous efforts have been made to bring the building, vineyards and equipment up to the highest level of architectural repair and viticultural ideals. There is every likelihood that the wine will be very exciting when the work starts to bear fruit.

The other property, Château St Pierre, is the subject of a cheering story of a dream come true. Many years ago, Henri Martin became the owner of **Château Gloria**, a good but unclassified growth in St Julien, which he transformed by hard work and unceasing activity into an internationally famous wine. For good measure, he started up and still enlivens a *commanderie* which holds very grand dinners at which princes, aristocrats and ambassadors are welcomed – provided that they swear that they will always support the cause of Bordeaux, and more specifically Médoc, wines. In 1982, Monsieur Martin got the chance to buy Château St Pierre, a classified growth somewhat run down, but an ideal object for the activity and attention of a man who so hates idleness.

St Julien is obviously a magic commune, not just for its quite wonderful wines!

ST JULIEN	
Outstanding Properties	**Excellent Properties**
Ducru Beaucaillou	Beychevelle
Gruaud Larose	Branaire Ducru*
Léoville Barton*	La Bridane*
Léoville Las Cases	Lagrange
Léoville Poyferré	St Pierre
*Can represent particular bargains	

Château Ducru Beaucaillou, one of the greatest wine properties in St Julien, was built above the cellars where the wine is kept.

PAUILLAC

As you travel north after passing Château Léoville Las Cases, the road crosses a stream which separates St Julien from Pauillac.

The first property, on the right, is **Château Latour**, which has a long drive up to its vat rooms and *chais*, passing on the way an elegant former pigeon loft, the tower of the château's name. Château Latour is owned by a British group, but it was a great favourite in England even before that link began. The château is a first growth, one of the four properties classified as such in 1855, to which Château Mouton Rothschild was later added. Château Latour has the reputation of being the longest-lasting of these properties in great years; the other side of the coin is that the wines 'open up', or become easy to taste, only at a later stage than others. The property also has a quite justified reputation for producing wines of first-rate quality in years when other châteaux can obtain nothing but mean wine from

Château Pichon Longueville Baron is a nineteenth-century concept of a Renaissance château, honoured in the 1855 classification.

their grapes. The tower which appears on the label can be seen from the road, but the house which goes with the property is rather disappointing. **Les Forts de Latour**, the second wine, is a somewhat faster-maturing version of its big brother.

Some of the many properties in this commune which should really be described here must be omitted for lack of space, but Château Latour's neighbour, **Château Pichon Longueville Lalande**, cannot be ignored; it is one of the risen stars of the appellation, producing wines of enormous charm and also – what is rarer – depth of taste. Its owner, Madame de Lencquesaing, is a woman of tremendous energy whose ambitions for her wine are reflected in its quality, and its price. Fortunately, you may sample some of the character of Pichon Lalande at half the price, by purchasing a bottle of the second wine, **Réserve de la Comtesse**.

There is another Château Pichon, **Château Pichon Longueville Baron**, which lies across the road from its near namesake and looks like an illustration from a nineteenth-century fairy tale, with turrets and steep roofs and, like all fairy-tale châteaux, no sign of life. Some would say that the same was true of the wine, but the property has recently changed hands and is likely to improve.

To one side of the main road there is a rising rather than risen star, **Château Grand Puy Lacoste**, which is run by the son of the magician who makes Château Ducru Beaucaillou. The first half-dozen vintages since he took charge have established the property as one of the finest wines of Pauillac, with some of the St Julien generosity.

Another exciting property is **Château Lynch Bages**, where an old-fashioned series of vat rooms and *chais* have been transformed into a hive of activity at all times of the year and where the number of tastings carried out each year must be as high as any where wine is made. Château Lynch Bages was classified in 1855, and its wine still shows the quality which would ensure classification today.

North of the town of Pauillac itself are the two remaining Médoc first growths, **Château Lafite Rothschild** and **Château Mouton Rothschild**. Château Mouton Rothschild is the property of the late Baron Philippe de Rothschild, who greatly influenced the wine trade, mainly because his insistence on château-bottling, starting in the 1920s, came at a time when this was not common. Even in the 1950s it was still possible to buy some first growths bottled otherwise than at the château. The Baron also introduced the delightful conceit of

The buildings of Château Lafite are at the centre of this fine estate in Pauillac. It is the most famous red wine in the world.

having a different label for each vintage and succeeded in persuading some very grand artists to make designs which would fit the long, thin strip across the top of the label which was all that was available. The Baron also fought a long campaign to have his property, classified as the first of the second growths of 1855, raised to the status of *Premier Cru*. His ultimate success brought about the only official revision of a much-debated classification.

The wines of Mouton Rothschild share with Latour an unwillingness to submit to early drinking: they are wines for decades rather than years of keeping and the best are among the greatest that will ever be drunk, with a huge colour when young, a strong, spicy bouquet which is said to be reminiscent of blackcurrants and power and length of taste.

The 1855 classification, following the confidence of the times, placed the growths it listed in exact order of quality. Château Lafite was, therefore, the first of the first growths and Château Margaux the second of the first growths. Such precision appears risible now, but the sheer subtlety of the greatest wines of Château Lafite demonstrates that the judges

may well have been right in 1855. Lafite lies spectacularly on a hill overlooking a meadow. There is a great sense of tradition, with son replacing father in various divisions of the running of the property, but the wines have perhaps changed in style more over the last 15 years than the other first growths, retaining Lafite's characteristic elegance and subtlety while apparently experimenting with the style of the wine they wished to produce. Not everyone has been impressed by the results.

PAUILLAC	
Outstanding Properties	**Excellent Properties**
Grand Puy Lacoste	Batailley*
Lafite Rothschild	Croizet Bages*
Latour	Duhart Milon
Lynch Bages	Forts de Latour* (second
Mouton Rothschild	wine of Ch. Latour)
	Mouton Baronne Philippe
*Can represent particular bargains	

St Estèphe

Just beyond Lafite the commune of St Estèphe, which also has its own appellation, begins. The first property is the most preposterous and entertaining building of the Médoc, housing the best wine of the commune, **Château Cos d'Estournel**. This nineteenth-century folly, a curious combination of Chinese pagoda and Islamic palace, is not a house but the *chais* and in it are a prodigious number of barrels kept in ideal conditions. This is another of the great châteaux of the Médoc, and the wine has a body and elegance which are the equal of any other Médoc property. This is the more remarkable since, with one or two exceptions, St Estèphe wines have a certain coarseness which prevents them attaining the very highest quality.

Of the other three classified growths of the commune, **Château Montrose** is one of the two best, made in a small village belonging to the property, with street names in white lettering on blue enamelled metal signs, just like the Champs Élysées. The wine here is generally deep coloured, with an intense, unyielding taste which develops quite slowly.

Among the less fashionable wines of St Estèphe, both **Cos Labory** and **Château de Pez** are consistently well made, if sometimes lacking finesse.

ST ESTÈPHE	
Outstanding Properties	**Excellent Properties**
Calon Ségur Cos d'Estournel Montrose	Le Crock* Houissant* Lafon Rochet Les Ormes de Pez* De Pez*
*Can represent particular bargains	

The chais *of Cos d'Estournel must be the most improbable wine-storing buildings anywhere. There is no château for the owners.*

THE NORTHERN MÉDOC

To the west and north of St Estèphe the appellation of the wines becomes again Haut Médoc. The parish of Cissac to the west contains several good vineyards, including the sturdy **Château Cissac** and the elegant **Château Hanteillan**. Heading north, you pass some excellent properties, including the well-known **Château Sociando Mallet**, a rising star, and **Château Coufran**, in the commune of St Seurin de Cadourne. The curiosity of this property is that it is planted almost entirely in the Merlot variety (so vulnerable to mildew), which is rarely seen in a concentration of more than 50 per cent elsewhere in the Haut Médoc.

St Seurin is separated from its northern neighbour, St Yzans de Médoc, by a stream, la Maréchale, which also acts as the boundary between the Haut Médoc and the Médoc. Curiously, the appreciable difference in the style of the wines does not necessarily correspond to a difference in quality: the

wines north of the Haut Médoc boundary are frequently from vineyards planted more extensively in the friendly Merlot variety, and if they lack the sterner qualities of claret (long-lasting ability and no insistence on obvious fruit) they make for very agreeable wines, more immediately pleasing to the consumer's palate than some of the grander wines from the Médoc.

One such agreeable wine comes from **Château Loudenne** (in the commune of St Yzans) and another, in Ordonnac, from **Château Potensac**, which regularly produces a delightful wine with just a hint of oak on the palate, stemming from the once common practice of storage in new barrels. This is claret of a high order, made by the owners of Léoville Las Cases.

Another example of excellent Médoc wine is **Château Patache d'Aux**, which is in the commune of Bégadan. This property provides a good example, also, of the technical improvements which winemakers who had worked in the former French colonies of North Africa brought with them on returning to France when those colonies won their independence in the early 1960s. These men and women introduced a standard of cleanliness in vat room and *chais* which, although one of the basic requirements of good winemaking, was often not present in the establishments they took over. Patache d'Aux is a wine with great elegance, which develops fairly fast in bottle.

From the same commune of Bégadan, **Château la Tour de By** produces sound wine, capable of considerable ageing.

The Médoc peninsula continues north, the vineyards give way to bleak, deserted and unproductive marshland and the traveller eventually arrives at the shores of the Atlantic Ocean. It seems a long way – and not merely in distance – from the ordered landscape of those world-famous châteaux, from the concerns and worries of the winemakers and the fluctuations and complexities of the international wine market.

OTHER NORTHERN MÉDOC WINES	
Leading Properties	
La Cardonne	Loudenne*
Coufran*	Patache d'Aux*
Greysac*	Tour de By*
*Can represent particular bargains	

THE MÉDOC CLASSIFICATION OF 1855, AS UPDATED IN 1973

PREMIERS CRUS (First growths)
(Placed in alphabetical order in 1973)

Château	Appellation
Château Lafite Rothschild	Pauillac
Château Latour	Pauillac
Château Margaux	Margaux
Château Mouton Rothschild	Pauillac
Château Haut Brion (the only Graves growth included in the 1855 classification)	Pessac

N.B. In the original classification, Château Mouton Rothschild was the first of the second growths rather than a first growth. At the same time that this château was promoted, the first growths of the Médoc were placed in alphabetical order. Previously, the order had been: Château Lafite, Château Margaux, Château Latour and Château Haut Brion.

SECONDS CRUS (Second growths)

Château	Appellation
Château Rausan Ségla	Margaux
Château Rauzan Gassies	Margaux
Château Léoville Las Cases	St Julien
Château Léoville Poyferré	St Julien
Château Léoville Barton	St Julien
Château Durfort Vivens	Margaux
Château Gruaud Larose	St Julien
Château Lascombes	Margaux
Château Brane Cantenac	Cantenac
Château Pichon Longueville Baron	Pauillac
Château Pichon Longueville Lalande	Pauillac
Château Ducru Beaucaillou	St Julien
Château Cos d'Estournel	St Estèphe
Château Montrose	St Estèphe

TROISIÈMES CRUS (Third growths)

Château	Appellation
Château Kirwan	Cantenac
Château d'Issan	Cantenac
Château Lagrange	St Julien
Château Langoa Barton	St Julien
Château Giscours	Labarde
Château Malescot St Exupéry	Margaux
Château Boyd Cantenac	Cantenac
Château Cantenac Brown	Cantenac
Château Palmer	Cantenac
Château la Lagune	Ludon
Château Desmirail	Margaux
Château Calon Ségur	St Estèphe
Château Ferrière	Margaux
Château Marquis d'Alesme Becker	Margaux

QUATRIÈMES CRUS (Fourth growths)

Château	Appellation
Château St Pierre	St Julien
Château Talbot	St Julien
Château Branaire Ducru	St Julien
Château Duhart Milon	Pauillac
Château Pouget	Cantenac
Château La Tour Carnet	St Laurent
Château Lafon Rochet	St Estèphe
Château Beychevelle	St Julien
Château Prieuré Lichine	Cantenac
Château Marquis de Terme	Margaux

CINQUIÈMES CRUS (Fifth growths)

Château	Appellation
Château Pontet Canet	Pauillac
Château Batailley	Pauillac
Château Haut Batailley	Pauillac
Château Grand Puy Lacoste	Pauillac
Château Grand Puy Ducasse	Pauillac
Château Lynch Bages	Pauillac
Château Lynch Moussas	Pauillac
Château Dauzac	Labarde
Château Mouton Baronne Philippe	Pauillac
Château du Tertre	Arsac
Château Haut Bages Libéral	Pauillac
Château Pédesclaux	Pauillac
Château Belgrave	St Laurent
Château Camensac	St Laurent
Château Cos Labory	St Estèphe
Château Clerc Milon	Pauillac
Château Croizet Bages	Pauillac
Château Cantemerle	Macau

GRAVES

The Graves is an appellation which is generally misunderstood, even by those who earn their livelihood by buying and selling wine. It covers a very large area, but only a small part of the land entitled to the appellation is in fact planted in vines: most is pine forest and a great amount of what is left over is devoted to houses, for the Graves surrounds both the city of Bordeaux and the town of Langon.

The area produces both red and white wines but, contrary to common belief, more red than white wine is made each year. In order to bring commercial value to the appellation, several innovations have been made. One was the introduction of a separate appellation, Graves Supérieures, which is, however, limited to full-bodied white wines. Another was the authorization in 1987 of a long-discussed appellation, Pessac & Léognan, for the wines, both red and white, which come from the best communes, sit-uated in the north of the appellation area. (The additional appellation with the Graves name, Graves de Vayres, is given to very modest wines from 50 km/30 miles away, across the river from Libourne.)

PESSAC & LÉOGNAN

The appellation Pessac & Léognan was created in 1987 after prolonged efforts to gain legal recognition for the superior qualities of the renowned properties in this northern section of the Graves. The appellation has comparable significance within the Graves to the village appellation of Margaux, for example, in the Médoc.

The wines from the three communes which comprise the region of Graves de Pessac include the most famous Graves wine, **Château Haut Brion**. This

Château Haut Brion was the only property outside the Médoc to be classified, as a first growth, in the 1855 classification.

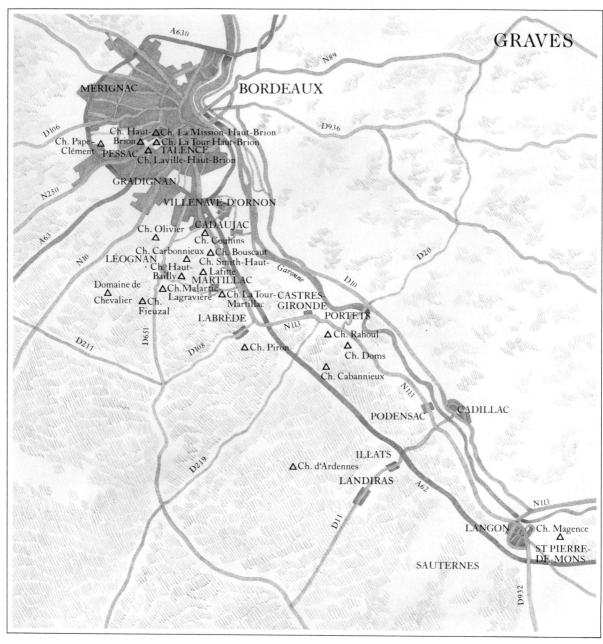

property was included in the famous classification of 1855 of the wines of the Médoc, which actually begins in present *appellation contrôlée* terms 6km/10 miles to the north of Haut Brion.

Haut Brion is one of the finest wines in the whole of Bordeaux, and well up to its position as one of the first growths, with Lafite, Latour, Margaux and, now, Mouton Rothschild. The property is in the middle of a town, Pessac, on the outskirts of Bordeaux, on land which must be the envy of every speculative builder in the city. The wine is always one of the most subtle wines of its vintage, and not a good

wine with which to start tasting claret: its subtlety, even in cask, is legendary and even in 'hard' years (years when the wine is aggressively tannic in the spring following the harvest) Haut Brion is persuasively elegant.

The same commune, Pessac, also has a more typical Graves, **Château Pape Clément**, which is a much bigger wine, good but rarely excellent and never subtle until it has been subjected to at least 20 years' ageing.

In Talence, one of the two other communes which form half of the new appellation Pessac & Léognan,

THE RED GRAVES CLASSIFICATION OF 1959	
These properties (not listed in order of merit) are now entitled to the appellation Pessac & Léognan.	
Property	**Commune**
La Mission Haut Brion	Talence
La Tour Haut Brion	Talence
Haut Brion	Pessac
Pape Clément	Pessac
Bouscaut	Cadaujac
Carbonnieux	Léognan
Domaine de Chevalier	Léognan
Fieuzal	Léognan
Haut Bailly	Léognan
Malartic Lagravière	Léognan
D'Olivier	Léognan
Smith Haut Lafitte	Martillac
La Tour Martillac	Martillac

Château la Mission Haut Brion lies across the road from Château Haut Brion, a short distance from the centre of the city of Bordeaux.

lies **Château la Mission Haut Brion**. This château was recently bought by the owners of Château Haut Brion. At least until the wines made by the new owners are sufficiently aged to be tasted thoroughly there will be a group of people who will compare their relative merits and divide themselves into partisans of either Haut Brion or of la Mission Haut Brion. The two wines were completely different, even though at one point the vineyards lie just on opposite sides of a busy road. The Mission has always had a depth of colour, a pronounced amount of tannin to make the mouth pucker up when tasted young, and such enormous power that it showed quite differently to the Haut Brion, with its great subtlety and understatement. The fact is that the two were, and will no doubt remain, impeccable wines made according to different standards by people as deeply attached to quality as it is possible to be.

The wine growers of Léognan have to fight for their land almost as much as those of Pessac, but the six communes which go to make up the group have considerably more acreage and a much greater variety of properties.

Just outside the town of Léognan, surrounded by trees, lies **Domaine de Chevalier**, which regularly produces one of the loveliest Graves wines which may, for the purposes of simplification, be equated with a major classified growth from the Médoc or one of the *Premiers Grands Crus* of St Emilion. Domaine de Chevalier is in all ways a curiosity, for it produces a first-rate white wine as well as the red and its location is so unsuited to growing vines, let alone

making great wine, that it is surprising that a severe frost has not more often done what it did in 1984, destroyed much of the vineyard. The character of Domaine de Chevalier is similar to Haut Brion at least in this, that it is made up of subtlety and elegance and that disagreeable young wines (which, like disagreeable children, may become very agreeable with age) seem never to be produced. The wines of Chevalier would have to be included in any group of ten major Bordeaux châteaux chosen to demonstrate to anyone who was in doubt that the red wines of Bordeaux are truly wonderful.

Among many other châteaux in the commune of Léognan, **Château Fieuzal** deserves a mention not only because of the impeccable condition of its *chais* but also because of its 'rounded' style. This style is due to a particular form of vinification (see pp.20-3) which, if comparison with what went before and what is tasted now is to be the criterion, is extremely successful. The question asked by the supporters of traditional vinification (in which the temperature is not allowed to go higher than 29°C/84°F) is whether wines made at a higher temperature will age as well. Whatever the answer to that question may be, the results can be highly desirable in the wine when young and there is no indication that the wines will not age attractively if allowed to.

Château Haut Bailly is another property in the commune of Léognan which regularly makes attractive wine in the best Graves tradition. It does not have the obvious 'backbone' of tannin which is perhaps most apparent in the austerity of some of the Pauillac wines, nor the concentration of the best St Emilions, but has an appealing straightforward elegance.

Among the other classified growths of Léognan, **Château Malartic Lagravière** makes rather more severe wine than the other wines of Léognan, with great lasting power, and the unclassified but attractive **Château Larrivet Haut Brion** also deserves a mention.

In the other communes which go to make up the Léognan group, Cadaujac has **Château Bouscaut**, which produces excellent wines now, and whose greatest old wines, from the 1920s, lasted for over 50 years without losing their character or their appeal to the palate.

In Martillac, there are two properties owned by groups connected with Bordeaux wine merchants, **Château Smith Haut Lafitte** and **Château la Tour Martillac**, both justifiably classified and on extremely well-situated land.

THE SOUTHERN GRAVES

The wines so far considered are very grand wines, whose price is naturally in accordance with their fame. South of Léognan, however, the vineyards are less well-known and more uneven in quality. The best can be very good, the least good are frankly bland or even coarse.

In the town of Castres, on the main road from Bordeaux to Langon, **Château Ferrande** lies near the river, although this is not immediately apparent from the road. The property is on good soil, the land sufficiently laced by streams to ensure good drainage. The wine, which is made from a mixture of Cabernet Franc, Cabernet Sauvignon and Merlot, is very fine indeed.

Somewhat to the south, in the commune of Portets, **Domaine la Grave** makes a red wine from Cabernet Sauvignon and Merlot which has the distinction natural to the first and the fruit characteristic of the second, helped, it must be said, by winemaking of the highest order.

What can be achieved as an economic proposition with a large property further south may be tasted at **Château Chantegrive**, a big property in Podensac, better known for its white than its red wine, but with a red which is extremely pleasing and which can be sold at a price which makes the cost of the famous wines of Graves appear outrageous.

Two properties situated in the southern Graves, near Langon, are owned by the winemaker and *négociant* Pierre Coste. These properties, **Domaine de Gaillat** and **Château Chicane**, make consistently attractive wine, excellent examples of high-temperature vinification.

Some years ago, confronted by merchants interested only in buying wine without great personality in bulk, some growers took to making a fresher wine, macerating the grapes before the fermentation proper started. The result was a wine with a bluish rim to it, a very pronounced bouquet of soft red fruit and a very agreeable taste. The problem was that the product was an excellent drink, but not altogether what is generally expected as wine. Experimentation over the years has allowed the problems to be ironed out (largely by using less of this specially vinified wine and more of the traditionally fermented wine blended together) and one of the most attractive in this style is **Château Cardaillan**, a wine made from land with the Graves appellation at Château de Malle, the Sauternes property in the commune of Preignac. The wine is fresh, stylish and good.

GRAVES		
Outstanding Properties	**Excellent Properties**	**Leading Properties**
Domaine de Chevalier Haut Brion La Mission Haut Brion	Bouscaut Fieuzal Haut Bailly Malartic Lagravière Smith Haut Lafitte	Chantegrive* Domaine de la Grave Ferrande Rahoul
*Can represent particular bargains		

ST EMILION AND POMEROL

St Emilion has the great advantage over the towns and villages of the Médoc and Graves of looking like a wine town even to those who have never seen one before. Its narrow streets are filled with shops devoted to selling wine, books about wine or objects in some way connected with wine. It is a town of steep alleys and from June till September it is packed and busy with tourists. In the winter it loses this activity except on Sundays, when the numerous and very good local restaurants are full of grandmothers being entertained to a long lunch by their sons and daughters while the grandchildren get more and more bored with the adults' incomprehensible willingness to waste a day at table.

This family side of life in the St Emilion and Pomerol area is apparent in the vineyards. Families are unwilling to part with their properties, or even to exchange one hectare for another: it is not unusual to find a major property which has been in the hands of a single family for well over 100 years without being enlarged or reduced by as much as a quarter of a hectare. There is a different mentality from that of the Médoc, and although it may have a stultifying effect on the social life of the area, it has certainly contributed to the enormous commercial success of the region over the last 30 years, which has seen the esteem and the price of the wines rise rapidly to the level of the better wines from the Médoc.

Whereas the Médoc is quite remarkably flat and the Graves region quite remarkably suburban in some parts and invaded by pine trees in others, the countryside around St Emilion is extremely varied.

St Emilion is a town of winding streets, built on a hillside on which some of the greatest wines of the region are grown. It looks just like most people imagine a wine town to be.

There are fine views over the valley of the Dordogne river which lies to the south of the ridge of hills on which the vineyards of St Emilion and Pomerol are found. The vineyards themselves look different, with a thinner density of vines to the hectare and a higher pruning system which looks less rigidly regimented than the Médoc's low pruning with its too-stunted arms. There is a great difference in the grape varieties planted, but that is not obvious to the eye, and varies from property to property. The soil also varies much more than in either the Médoc or the Graves and cannot be regarded as the unifying factor of the various St Emilion appellations (which include the main region of St Emilion and the various surrounding villages – the satellites – which incorporate St Emilion in their name). The variations in soil within the St Emilion constellation are said to be at least five, and the fact that one of the eight communes (that of St Emilion itself) has all but two of the classified growths, although it has all five variations of soil within its boundaries, is some indication of the differences which exist in the finer characteristics of the wines and in the sheer quality of the whole.

Although the significance of soil will be dealt with when individual properties are mentioned, it should be said here that many tasters have suggested that St Emilion should be divided into two or even three appellations rather than including, as it does at present, wines of a markedly different style, coming from quite different soils.

A division into two would not be one of quality, but of style. It would divide those wines made on the plateau at the top of the hill in the town of St Emilion from those made on the slopes running south, towards the river. Wine-merchants refer to these different areas as St Emilion Graves and St Emilion Côtes. The former comes from various soils similar at least in that they have a high gravel/pebble content, and are on the plateau which stretches from the top of the town of St Emilion to Pomerol; the 'Graves' of the name refers to the soil and has no other connection with the area south of the city of Bordeaux. The latter, which also includes a variety of soils, has the common feature of being situated on hilly land. If there were a third division, it would separate one group of properties making rather undistinguished wine, situated on low-lying land near the Dordogne. This is rich alluvial soil between the river and St Emilion, making wine which is only distantly related in quality to the greatest wines of the plateau or the *côtes* (hills).

Indeed, these wines from alluvial soil are closer in style to those of the minor St Emilion appellations, the so-called 'satellite' villages of Lussac St Emilion, Puisseguin St Emilion, Montagne St Emilion and St Georges St Emilion. If one could argue for a sub-division of the main St Emilion region into two, it would be equally sensible to group these outlying districts under a single appellation of St Emilion Villages. They share a rusticity, a simple earthy appeal, which does not vary greatly from one village to the next. There is greater potential in the region of Fronsac, separated from St Emilion by the Isle river, and in Pomerol's less grand neighbour, Lalande de Pomerol.

Pomerol itself has always very wisely resisted the

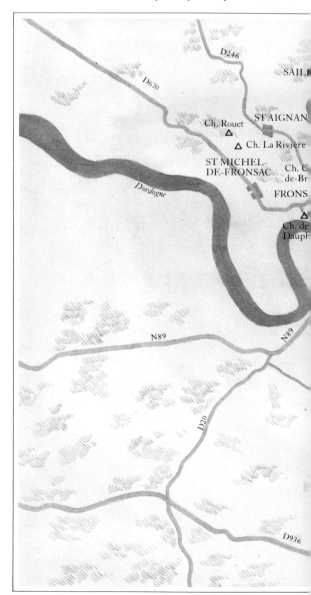

urge to have a classification made of its wines. The absence of such an official ranking has not had the effect of reducing the reputation or price of the wines to a uniform level (far from it), nor has it limited the interest in increasing quality within the 'appellation', but it has avoided a number of difficulties which the recent classifications of St Emilion seem to have brought in their wake.

Unlike the top wines of the Médoc and Sauternes, those of St Emilion were not classified in 1855, but the local proprietors eventually decided to have a disinterested classification made in 1954. The fact that the I.N.A.O. carried it out gave it the legal force of an *appellation contrôlée* when it was published in 1955. The highest class – *Premier Grand Cru* – was headed by Château Cheval Blanc and Château Ausone, unquestionably the outstanding properties of the appellation, and there was general consensus among growers and other wine people that the other nine properties in this class were also worthy of their rank. There was, however, a general impression that the two grandest of the wines should have had a special position and title. Outside St Emilion it was felt that the second group of the 1955 classification, 63 châteaux entitled to describe themselves as *Grand Cru Classé*, included too many properties.

The terms of the original classification called for a periodic revision, also by the I.N.A.O. The first such revision appeared in 1969, when the group of 12 *Premiers Crus*, headed by Château Cheval Blanc

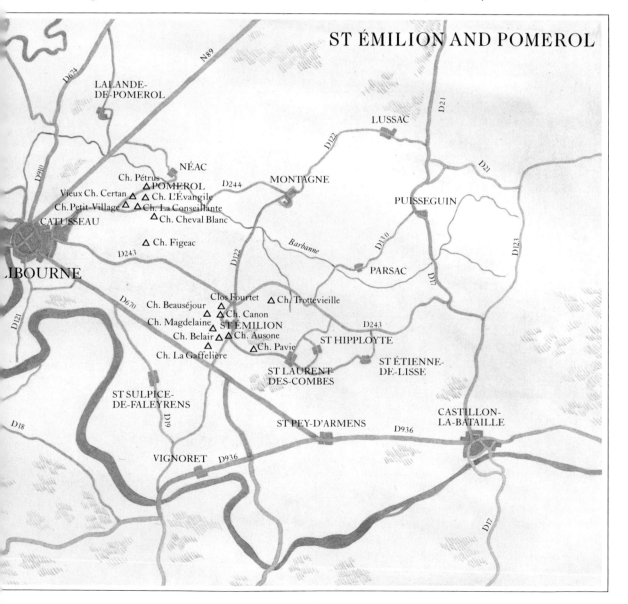

and Ausone, was left unaltered, but a total of 73 properties were listed as entitled to the rank of *Grand Cru*. In 1986, however, a new classification demoted Château Beau Séjour (as one of the two divisions of the original Château Beauséjour had chosen to be called) from the rank of *Premier Cru* and made various other alterations which cut the number of *Grands Crus Classés* back to 63. As the local newspaper suggested, this was a severe pruning, and it was not greeted with universal agreement, even outside the area covered by the appellation.

The division of the St Emilion classification into *Premiers Crus* and *Grands Crus* has a comparative democracy and apparent simplicity, lacking in the five-tier 1855 classification of the Médoc. Unfortunately, this clarity is ruined by the coexistence of the confusing appellation 'St Emilion Grand Cru', which has nothing to do with the classification. On the contrary, it is an indication of merit to which any St Emilion property may aspire by conforming to certain qualitative requirements and passing an annual tasting test. The description does *not* mean that the property is one of the classified growths, which indicate their hereditary aristocracy by the addition of one vital word to their designation: 'St Emilion Grand Cru Classé'.

ST EMILION (GRAVES)

As you drive 3km/2 miles east from the town of Libourne, you pass through some well-known Pomerol vineyards on both sides of the road and then come upon St Emilion properties on the right. The left continues to be Pomerol. This part of the commune of St Emilion is often referred to as St Emilion (Graves).

At blind tastings of the wines of major châteaux it is not uncommon for experienced and wary tasters to mark St Emilion wines as Margaux and vice versa. When they do this, the St Emilion wine is generally one from this Graves area, where the soil is similar to that of the Médoc, with the excellent drainage given by pebbles and chips of hard rock enabling extensive root development which allows the vine to absorb various trace elements from the subsoil.

The most famous property in this part of the commune is **Château Cheval Blanc**, which is a handsome creamy white house in a small wooded garden in the middle of a fine single parcel of what is one of the best vineyards in the world. The vineyards are planted very largely in Cabernet Franc, the remaining third being Merlot. The terrain is not hilly, but

Château Cheval Blanc is one of the two outstanding châteaux in the St Emilion appellation contrôlée, *and is surrounded by a sea of gently undulating, immaculately tended vines.*

there are appreciable variations of height and as early as the nineteenth century the owners began draining the land, which has a clay subsoil. The greatest vintages of Cheval Blanc give the lie to those who claim that St Emilion wines do not age as well as those of the Médoc. They seem to have a full-bodied character, which makes them clearly St Emilion when tasted with awareness of the producing château, but which still fools anyone who has not caught sight of the label.

Château Cheval Blanc is one of the three largest of the *Premiers Grands Crus Classés* of St Emilion. Its neighbour, separated by a narrow road at one point, is **Château Figeac**. It is unusual in the Bordelais to find a large property which is very much the reflection of one man. There are good winemakers and bad in the area and their names are well-known, but there are very few who are so completely identified with their property. Thierry Manoncourt has lavished care and time, almost all his time, on his Château Figeac and he regularly produces one of the out-

standing wines of the appellation. If any one of the red wine producers of the Libournais can claim to understand why they make such good wine at their particular property it is Monsieur Manoncourt. One of the reasons which he advances for the quality of Figeac is the extremely unusual mixture of grapes, for a third of the vineyard is planted in Cabernet Sauvignon, in addition to a third in Cabernet Franc and another in Merlot. The reason for this is that the soil at Figeac is particularly and unusually rich in pebbles or *graves*, similar to those encountered in the Médoc. Such soil is better suited to the Cabernet Sauvignon than the other soils of the St Emilion appellation. What baffles the outsider is that the wine still has the characteristics of a St Emilion.

If these two properties are the only two *Premiers Grands Crus* in this part of St Emilion, there are other excellent vineyards which regularly produce wine that is among the best of the large league of classified growths. One rising star is **Château la Dominique**, which adjoins Cheval Blanc to the east and

Château Figeac is a highly esteemed property lying on an unusual outcrop of pebble soil,
on the plâteau of St Emilion. Cabernet Sauvignon, Cabernet Franc and Merlot are all grown here.

which produces a wine of great elegance, unfortunately still at a price beyond the reach of most. **Château Croque-Michotte** is a *Grand Cru* which is worth looking out for and is usually available at a more acceptable price. It is a wine which repays some ageing, being less attractive when recently bottled than those mentioned above. Another property which is well worth seeking out, and can be drunk rather younger than its grander neighbours, is **Château Montlabert**, a delicate wine carefully made.

ST EMILION (GRAVES)	
Outstanding Properties	**Excellent Properties**
Cheval Blanc Figeac	La Dominique De Grand Corbin* Soutard* La Tour Figeac*
*Can represent particular bargains	

THE ST EMILION CLASSIFICATION OF 1986

PREMIERS GRANDS CRUS CLASSÉS	GRANDS CRUS CLASSÉS	
A Ausone Cheval Blanc **B** Beauséjour (Duffau-Lagarosse) Belair Canon Clos Fourtet Figeac La Gaffelière Magdelaine Pavie Trottevieille	L'Angélus L'Arrosée Balestard la Tonnelle Beau-Séjour (Bécot) Bellevue Bergat Berliquet Cadet Piola Canon la Gaffelière Cap de Mourlin Le Châtelet Chauvin Clos des Jacobins Clos la Madeleine Clos de l'Oratoire Clos St Martin La Clotte La Clusière Corbin Corbin Michotte Couvent des Jacobins Croque-Michotte Curé Bon Dassault La Dominique Faurie de Souchard Fomplégade Fonroque Franc Mayne Grand Barrail Lamarzelle Figeac Grand Corbin Grand Corbin Despagne Grand Mayne Grand Pontet Guadet St Julien Haut Corbin Haut Sarpe	Laniote Larcis-Ducasse Lamarzelle Larmande Laroze Matras Mauvezin Moulin du Cadet L'Oratoire Pavie Decesse Pavie Macquin Pavillon Cadet Petit Faurie de Soutard Le Prieuré Ripeau Sansonnet St Georges Côte Pavie La Serre Soutard Tertre Daugay La Tour du Pin Figeac (Giraud- Bélivier) La Tour du Pin Figeac (Vignobles Moueix) La Tour Figeac Trimoulet Troplong Mondot Villemaurine Yon Figeac

St Emilion (Côtes)

The pebbly/gravelly soil of St Emilion (Graves) can readily be made out from aerial photographs and the stones admired in the *chais* of Château Figeac. The nature of the soil and even the subsoil in the hilly part of St Emilion – the Côtes – is much easier to discern, however, at its finest vineyard, **Château Ausone**. This is, of course, one of the two properties bracketed together as the first of the *Premiers Crus* in all the St Emilion classifications.

Ausone is the French form of the Latin Ausonius, the Gallo-Roman poet who wrote about the region but probably had nothing to do with the present estate. The vineyards are on steep slopes, the Côte de la Magdelaine, on a limestone subsoil which has been hollowed out at Château Ausone to make a cave-cellar, just as it has, even more surprisingly, at Clos Fourtet. The cellar at Ausone was originally quarried to provide building stone for the town of St Emilion, which lies below. Ausone is a small property, and produces wines always remarkable for their limpidity and subtlety from a mixture of half Cabernet Franc and half Merlot vines. They age extremely well and, indeed, need many years to develop their remarkable complexity. The neighbouring **Château Belair**, owned by the same family, is in no way the second wine of Ausone, but shares some of its finesse without having quite the same power or longevity. The present high reputation of both properties reflects the talent of Pascal Delbeck, their gifted young manager.

In the same part of St Emilion is **Château Magdelaine**, on the same chalky clay soil which would, on flat ground, give high production. It highlights the significance of drainage that production of this elegant wine, even from the normally generous Merlot in which this property is widely planted, is in rather small quantity. This is a very fine *Premier Cru* and the wine is made with great care by Jean Claude Berrouet, who is one of the most consistently excellent vinifiers in the St Emilion-Pomerol region, overseeing a large number of properties controlled by the Moueix family of Libourne.

Château Canon is a large *Premier Cru* by St Emilion standards, with 18 hectares of well-situated land. In a period of stainless steel vats, the property has settled for wooden fermenting vats and the results over the last half dozen years have been extremely successful, giving a wine with more body and above all a more complex and attractive taste than during the early 1970s, when the property had a series of rather undistinguished wines. The most important factor in this improvement, however, is the personal enthusiasm and care of Eric Fournier, who now manages the estate on behalf of his family.

The adaptability of wines is well illustrated by what happens at Canon in shallow soil, with a chalky subsoil. Instead of penetrating deep, as is the case in the Médoc, the vines here develop a horizontal root system. It is for this reason that the number of vines per hectare is less in the region than in the Médoc.

Another renowned *Premier Cru* (which is situated, like all the others, within the commune of St Emilion itself) is **Château Pavie**, lying to the south of the town. The largest of the *Premiers Crus*, it is extensive enough to have several types of soil. The vineyards face south, on a fairly severe slope, and regularly produce wine which immediately commands respect from a taster but which, in a year with insufficient sun, can lack the full-bodied attractiveness which attaches to the appellation. The property has a high percentage (25 per cent) of Cabernet Sauvignon, which goes some way to explain both its profundity of taste and occasional lack of charm.

Château la Gaffelière is a *Premier Cru* which can produce excellent wines, usually somewhat less fine but more immediately attractive than Pavie. It shares with Pavie the tendency to vary in quality rather more than the other *Premiers Crus* of the 'Côtes'. Some sign of what the property can produce at its best is given by the 1975 vintage, one of the outstanding wines from this very mixed year.

For those with well-lined pockets, there are three other *Premiers Grands Crus Classés*: **Châteaux Beauséjour, Trottevieille** and **Clos Fourtet**.

Within the group of classified growths, other than the *Premiers Crus* already mentioned, there are a great many very fine wines, but they suffer from being made in such small quantities that they are difficult to find. It is for this reason that the following comments are restricted to vineyards of 10 hectares or more, which may be expected to produce 50,000 bottles a year and be offered for sale in more than one country.

On the direct but winding road from Libourne to St Emilion there are two good properties on the right-hand side, descending from the plateau to the Dordogne river at a rather less severe incline than that on which Ausone is situated. These are l'Angélus and Grand Mayne.

Château l'Angélus is well situated on land which faces south, and is planted half in Merlot, half in Cabernet Franc. It has for the last 20 years produced

*Classified with Château Cheval Blanc as the glories of St Emilion,
Château Ausone is built on a thick chalk cliff and has cellar space
hollowed out of the stone.*

big, attractive wines which are much enjoyed as being richer and more obviously appealing than most Graves or Médoc wines. What is interesting is that the success of the property over that period has encouraged the use of new oak barrels since 1980. Whether this very serious effort to improve the wine (new oak barrels are extremely expensive) will alter the basic style, as seems probable, remains to be seen as the wines become ready to drink. (The effect of oak on young wine is very great and masks the true nature of the wine. It is only after some years of ageing that the total effect becomes clear.)

Château Grand Mayne also lies on the slopes facing south and is a delightful seventeenth-century house, now restored to youth. The wines are vinified in stainless steel and part of the crop is kept in new oak, to add the hint of vanilla or oak which is so popular with consumers at the moment. The result is a wine of great distinction, with more subtlety and

less body than the Angélus. Just south of St Emilion is a property which has attracted much attention over the last few years in particular: **Château l'Arrosée**. The vineyard is planted one third with Cabernet Sauvignon, which may give it the individuality it shows at blind tastings of St Emilions. The site of the property, on the lower slopes before the plain of alluvial soil, is also a good one. The wine, in any case, has an extremely interesting and complex taste.

Just outside St Emilion, to the other side of the town, is **Château Balestard la Tonnelle**, which consistently makes wine of high quality. The style is of deep-coloured, full-bodied wines which have great complexity as well.

To the south-east of the town, **Château Troplong Mondot** is at the peak of an impressive hill by Gironde standards, which are not exactly those of a mountainous area. The vineyards are well situated to make excellent wines and that is what the owners are trying to bring about. They have started, as is often the case, by revamping the label. Until the late 1970s the wines tended to be slightly coarse, although with good colour and much fruit. This seems to be changing as they take on the more austere character which goes with wines of greater distinction before they have aged sufficiently.

The St Emilion wines not included in the classification do not generally have the same depth or complexity of taste as those that have been described above, but they can be more easily afforded and come from a very distinguished background.

Keeping the same criterion of a vineyard of more than 10 hectares, the following are some of the wines worth noting:

Château Billerond is made by the *cave coopérative* of St Emilion, which bears the name Union des Producteurs and is a very big, efficient organization. It is one of many individual wines produced and its origin can be recognized by the line *mise en bouteille à la propriété* rather than *mise en bouteille au château* on the label. This is good wine at a fair price. It is not for laying down for many years.

Château Bellefont Belcier is in the commune of St Laurent des Combes, which adjoins St Emilion and slopes down towards the Dordogne to the south. This is an attractive wine, young, light and sound, with a distinct presence of the Merlot grape variety. Again, not for laying down.

In St Etienne de Lisse, a commune to the east of St Laurent des Combes, also on a hill, is **Château Bernateau** or **Côtes Bernateau**, which produces 80,000 bottles of good, rather light St Emilion.

Perhaps the best of the communes whose wines have the right to use the appellation is St Christophe des Bardes, east of the town of St Emilion, on mainly chalky soil in hilly countryside out of sight of the Dordogne river. One property whose wine is often seen is **Château Fombrauge**, where the judicious

ST EMILION (CÔTES)	
Outstanding Properties	**Excellent Properties**
Ausone	L'Arrosée
Belair	Balestard la Tonnelle*
Magdelaine	Billerond*
Pavie	Bonnet Canon
	La Gaffelière
	Grand Mayne*
*Can represent particular bargains	

Although Libourne is less than 30 km/20 miles from Bordeaux, it has a wine world of its own, and is a centre for the 'right bank' wines (Pomerol, St Emilion and the other appellations in the immediate area).

use of new oak for about a quarter of each harvest adds a hint of complexity which might otherwise be missing.

Another property in the commune is **Château Lapelletrie**, where the owners make sound wine for drinking within three years of bottling.

St Pey d'Armens is at one corner of a triangle of land between the N670 (the perfectly straight road between Libourne and St Pey d'Armens) and the Dordogne river, where what is least attractive in the St Emilion appellation is made. **Château Bonnet**, however, which is owned and run by the Bonnet family, is made on several soils and produces an attractive and individual wine.

THE MINOR ST EMILION APPELLATIONS

Long ago, there was a *Jurade* of St Emilion, a town council whose jurisdiction extended well beyond the walls of the town of St Emilion itself. The communes other than St Emilion which now have the right to the *appellation contrôlée* St Emilion for their wines also came under the jurisdiction of the *Jurade* but so, too, did other communes. There were originally five which were allowed to add St Emilion to their name. In 1973 two of these, Parsac and St Georges, were linked with Montagne St Emilion administratively, in a single commune. They nonetheless retain the right to use the names Parsac St Emilion or St Georges St Emilion if they wish, since the laws of *appellation contrôlée* were not changed because of the administrative re-shuffling.

All the communes under discussion lie between 10 and 25 km/6 and 15 miles north-east of St Emilion.

In 1986, Lussac St Emilion declared the equivalent of some 700,000 bottles of its appellation, Montagne St Emilion 850,000, Puisseguin 40,000 and St Georges St Emilion about 100,000. No proprietor in Parsac declared under that appellation.

These wines are not without quality, and some good properties are listed below. On the whole,

however, they are not in the same class as the wines which have just been described (see p. 58 onwards). When they do stand out it is because they have been made with great care by a good winemaker. As elsewhere, this becomes apparent in the irregularity of quality from year to year. No one would pretend that a classified growth was of equal quality in every vintage, but there is a minimum quality which a major property can sustain but which a small property in a lesser appellation can only achieve in the most exceptional years.

Like all five communes, Lussac has a variety of soils and subsoils, with a tendency to become heavier and richer in clay towards the boundaries where they give way to the basic appellation of Bordeaux Supérieur or Bordeaux Côtes de Castillon.

In Lussac, **Château Lyonnat** is the biggest property, and is indeed very large. It makes full-bodied wines which are agreeable but lacking in finesse.

Château Courlat and **Château Tour de Grenet** are other quite large estates which produce wines that are sufficiently widely distributed to be worth mentioning. Neither is great, but both are sound.

In Montagne St Emilion (the new Montagne St Emilion which includes Parsac and most of St Georges St Emilion), **Château Calon** is a worthy wine, big in good years and vinified to last. **Château Grand Barril** is a rather lighter wine, made by the pupils of the *lycée agricole* (professional secondary school). **Château la Papeterie** (literally 'paper-mill') is an improbably named but good growth which you may also find.

POMEROL

The commune of Pomerol lies to the north-east of Libourne. If you drive through Libourne from Bordeaux to get there, you pass through a stretch of ribbon development before getting to the vineyards. There is no town of Pomerol, no centre to what has become one of the most famous *appellations contrôlées*. Pomerol is a somewhat amorphous commune and the boundary between part of it and St Emilion is at one stage no more than a road, an arbitrary border which might encourage anyone who did not know the wines of Pomerol to believe that there was no coherent element in the appellation.

This apparent lack of uniformity goes further: the varieties in soil type within the commune are extreme, from heavy, cold clay to quick-draining sandy soil.

THE MINOR ST EMILION APPELLATIONS	
Leading Properties	
Calon	La Papeterie
Courlat	Macquin St Georges
Grand Barril	Tour de Grenet
Lyonnat	

Château Pétrus is a small property with an uninspiring house but has a reputation which is second to none amongst the wines of Bordeaux.

Even more, the winemakers in the commune are not united in any common tradition of vinification: the small size of some of the properties, which would be hopelessly uneconomic in an area where wine sold for a lesser price, allows quite remarkable systems of vinification to thrive: some wines are kept for an amazing five weeks in vat to macerate with the solid matter after the fermentation, others are so macerated during the vinification that less than a week is deemed sufficient to produce a wine of which the owner is quite proud.

Yet the appellation has a real identity, however difficult that is to explain. One of the common factors is the extensive planting of the Merlot grape. Another is perhaps the similarity, throughout the commune, of the microclimate: almost all the commune is on the same, very slightly undulating parcel of land, without huge plantations of trees which might also introduce microclimates for individual properties.

Another of the main reasons for the distinctive identity of the wines produced within the commune is probably the extremely unusual similarity in the age of the vines and their common origin. When the fierce frosts of February 1956 killed off so many vines and made it a wiser decision to grub up entire vineyards rather than fill in the gaps, the whole commune had to replant and there is therefore an unusual unity of grape variety, source and age.

The replanting after the 1956 frosts is one of the three steps in the rise of the commune. The other two have also occurred since the war, and are intimately related. They are the inclusion of Pomerol as a wine-producing area in the small number of names known to connoisseurs throughout the world; and the rise in status of Château Pétrus, which can now challenge any other property in the whole Bordeaux area. The rise of Pétrus has done a great deal for Pomerol, the rise of Pomerol as much for Pétrus.

Describing Pomerols as a group is best approached by insisting on the concentration of flavour and the very pronounced presence of fruit in the wines. There are wonderfully elegant Pomerols, but unlike an elegant Médoc, they have a reserve, for this taster at least, of concentrated fruit rather than, as in the Médoc, of greater subtlety and complexity.

It is sometimes suggested that Pomerol is a half-way stage between the Médoc and Burgundy. This remark has the attraction of all nicely turned phrases, but it does no justice to the greatest wines which are made (mostly) from the Cabernet Sauvignon variety (in the Médoc), the Pinot Noir (in Burgundy) and the Merlot (in Pomerol). If, as an American writer suggested, wine is the grape's bid for immortality, Pomerol is the Merlot's best claim to be a maker of great wines.

Château Pétrus in many ways dominates Pomerol and it is a wine of such enormous complexity that it deserves to be treated at some length, although it is only *primus inter pares*, since there is no official classification of the wines that are produced by the commune.

The property is situated on a small, round patch of clay soil with a small proportion of gravel. This is not the soil of which grape-growers or winemakers dream, for the roots cannot penetrate the tightly packed clay any more than the water can. On such gently sloping land as the 12 hectares the property possesses, drainage is an even greater and more permanently pressing problem than elsewhere, and it is fair to say that both here and at Château Yquem

*Vieux Château Certan, one of the leading Pomerol
vineyards, has a seventeenth-century château which is more dignified
than the modest houses usually found in the region.*

(the great sweet white wine-producing property
50 km/30 miles to the south), it is the enormous care
and effort given by successive generations rather
than natural features which make the wine so great.

Statistics are as boring in wine matters as elsewhere, but there are some quite remarkable figures
which deserve reflection and respect. The average
age of the vines is over 40 years, which is a handsome
age by any standards of grape growing, but the more
remarkable when the enforced replanting after the
1956 frosts are taken into account.

The intention of the present owners is to replant
only after the vines have been planted for 75 years.
Since vines give less wine as they grow older, albeit
of higher quality, this is a token of the effort
expended on quality. The property also has the great
advantage of being managed by the Moueix family
which controls a number of related properties and
can therefore call on a large team of pickers. As a
result the entire crop can be picked, if necessary, in a
day. This is a luxury which every grower must envy,

for a hint of a cloud in the sky can encourage the
winemaker at Pétrus to harvest before the rain.

Pétrus has 5 per cent of its vineyards under Cabernet Franc, the rest under Merlot. The wines are
vinified in vitrified cement vats and they are followed
with enormous care until they are bottled and leave
the property. It is a nice irony that this mighty
château possesses not a castle but a modest house.

The neighbouring property, **Vieux Château Certan**, has a fine house worthy of being called both
château and *vieux*. Successive owners have adopted a
way of making a wine that is quite distinct from their
neighbour's. The most obvious difference is in the
varieties of grapes planted: Merlot accounts for only
half the vineyard area, Cabernet Franc for 25 per
cent, Cabernet Sauvignon for 20 per cent, with 5 per
cent of Malbec for good measure. The result is a
wine with less colour and concentration, but more
obviously charming and with greater subtlety than
elsewhere in the commune.

Between Vieux Château Certan and the village of

POMEROL	
Outstanding Properties	**Leading Properties**
La Conseillante L'Evangile Petit Village Pétrus Vieux Ch. Certan	Beauregard* Certan de May Lagrange* Nenin La Pointe
*Can represent particular bargains	

Pomerol-Catusseau lies **Château Petit Village**, which regularly produces a wine with more body than Vieux Château Certan, and which shows extremely well while still in cask. The three wines represent only part of the variety of Pomerol wines, but they share that most difficult quality to find in a wine, consistent and obvious distinction.

Slightly nearer Libourne than Petit Village is another big property by the standards of Pomerol, **Château Nenin**. This is a property which has always produced sound wines, but either the land will not give subtle wine or the men who make it prefer a deep-coloured wine with a certain coarseness.

The biggest of the Pomerol properties, **Château de Sales**, has been in the same family for 400 years and the château itself is a handsome building. The wine, the most commonly met of the Pomerol growths because of the high production from more than 50 hectares, is sound, but not among the greatest Pomerol names. The wines here are inclined to mature rather faster than the more famous growths and to be rather less attractive in poor vintages.

No account of Pomerol, however brief, would be complete without mention of two properties which lie next to each other, just across the road from Château Cheval Blanc of St Emilion. From land as nearly identical in constitution, disposition to the sun and slope as possible, they produce two such different wines that only variations in the age of the vines, the varieties planted and winemaking techniques can explain them: **l'Evangile**, huge in colour and body and difficult to taste until somewhat aged, and the **Conseillante**, with great power but a certain lack of depth.

LALANDE DE POMEROL

A stream, the Brabanne, separates Pomerol from its 'satellite' appellation, Lalande de Pomerol.

Lalande de Pomerol produces rather more wine than Pomerol in most years. Its finest wines do not, of course, equal the best from its neighbour, but they challenge and sometimes even outstrip the least good of Pomerol. This is a varied appellation, with several types of soil, a hillier countryside and, in the parts furthest from the Brabanne boundary, some rather undistinguished wine. The appellation is worth investigating, however, not least because this can be done at less than the sometimes very high cost of examining the wines of Pomerol itself. The *appellation contrôlée* covers two communes, Lalande de Pomerol and Néac. Néac once used its own commune name, which was a proper *appellation contrôlée* in its own right. Even the most parochially minded winemakers of Néac have now ceased to declare their wine as Néac, and in 1986 all the wine of the commune was declared as Lalande de Pomerol, an eloquent reminder of the significance of the name Pomerol in the eyes of the consumer.

Château Bertineau St Vincent is an excellent wine from the region, made by a sensitive winemaker. One of the interesting features of the property is that its owner also owns the Pomerol property **Château le Bon Pasteur**, which is one of the best-known Pomerols in the lower price range, grown in unexciting land on the border between Pomerol and St Emilion. The Lalande de Pomerol has less depth and length than the Pomerol, but a very fruity, open bouquet makes an immediately attractive impression which continues throughout.

A better-known property in the appellation is **Château des Annereaux**, which is in the commune of Lalande. The property is a large one, and produces a wine with less obvious charm than the Bertineau, but of great regularity of quality from one year to another.

Another vineyard making sufficient wine to be distributed widely is **Château Haut Surget** in Néac. This is obviously attractive wine, not vinified for laying down but rather for drinking within five years of the harvest.

If you are touring in the area, the church of Lalande de Pomerol is worth a detour. On the other hand, the church of Pomerol itself is of little interest but can be admired when seen across the flat land in which it lies.

LALANDE DE POMEROL
All the wines mentioned here come from leading properties.

FRONSAC

On the western side of the Isle river, which joins the Dordogne at Libourne, is the Fronsadais, an area of land which takes its name from the village of Fronsac. The vineyards with the name Fronsac in their *appellation contrôlée* lie to the right of the main N670 road as it runs west along the Dordogne from Libourne to St André de Cubzac. The road runs at first at the foot of what appear to be cliffs, with one hill, the Tertre de Fronsac, looking much higher than the 80 m/250 ft the map indicates.

This is fine country, well worth exploring for its visual beauty and the lovely Romanesque churches. These are built in the handsome local stone which is at the top of the hills, on the slopes of which the best vineyards, those with the appellation Canon Fronsac, are situated. The land to the south of the N670 is almost entirely alluvial soil, and only has the right to the appellation Bordeaux.

In the eighteenth century Fronsac wines were better known, and sold for a higher price, than the wines of Pomerol or St Emilion. It has been suggested by the great geographer and historian of the region, Henry Enjalbert, that the reason for the wine's subsequent decline was greed: encouraged by the success of the excellent wine made on the slopes facing south, the producers took to planting vines also on the much richer alluvial soil and made a handsome profit at the cost of lowering the quality and renown of their region.

There are two appellations in use in this small area, Canon Fronsac and Fronsac. The usage of Côtes de Canon Fronsac, which described the geographical origin of the wines it covered, has gone out of fashion but is worth remembering as an indication that Canon Fronsac wines come from the slopes and produce generally better wines than those from the lower-lying land which are designated simply as Fronsac.

The Canon Fronsac appellation is limited to the communes of St Michel de Fronsac and parts of Fronsac. The Fronsac appellation covers all or part of six communes, St Aignan, La Rivière, St Germain la Rivière, Saillans, Galgon and part of Fronsac.

Both appellations are making a considerable and concerted effort to improve their wines and it will be interesting to see how successful they are. The major improvement will be the slowest: the planting of a wider range of grape varieties than the Merlot which at present covers so great a part of every vineyard. The two appellations have sufficient evident potential to encourage improvements by other methods, however, and limitations on production and trial by tasting may well be having a desirable effect already.

Château Villars, in the commune of Saillans,

produces an attractive wine, part aged in new oak, which has as much depth of taste as many wines of more famous appellations and which is also extremely consistent in quality. Very close by, **Château Dalem** produces wines which also win prizes, with slightly less friendly qualities when young, but with excellent ageing characteristics.

Both the above properties are on the edge of the plateau and the slopes and so, at the other end of the Fronsac appellation line of communes, is **Château Rouet**. The wine here is more delicate, with a more obviously charming bouquet and immediate attack.

This is an area of handsome châteaux which approximate what most of us expect a château to be. **Château de la Dauphine**, in Fronsac, is one of the loveliest of the smaller buildings, designed by Victor Louis, the region's most famous eighteenth-century architect. The wine is well-balanced and of some complexity, part aged in oak.

Another very handsome wine-producing château in the Fronsadais, though of a less sober design, is **Château la Rivière**, in the commune of that name. Its origins go back to the thirteenth century, but it is its unrestrained appeal to nineteenth-century romantic taste which draws the eye now. In vinous terms, this is a very big Fronsac property and it makes excellent Fronsac which ages quite quickly. It is possible to visit the cellars.

Among the wines of Canon Fronsac which are worth looking out for, **Château Canon de Brem**

Fronsac is set in delightful countryside, with small villages and exciting views. The wines were at one time more sought-after than those of Pomerol and the Médoc.

produces one of the most exciting. It is one of three properties (La Dauphine and Canon Moueix are the others), which have been bought by the Moueix family of Libourne, part-owners of Château Pétrus and proprietors of a string of other famous properties in Pomerol and St Emilion. Their interest in developing the wines of Fronsac bodes well for the future of this appellation.

FRONSAC

All the wines mentioned on pages 70-2 represent good value at the time of writing; few other properties in the Fronsac region are sufficiently established to be able to produce first-rate wines on a regular basis.

Château la Rivière is an incredibly ornate building set high on the cliff overlooking the Dordogne river, in Fronsac. The origins reach as far back as the thirteenth century.

BLAYE, BOURG AND THE
PREMIÈRES CÔTES DE BORDEAUX

Three regions of *appellation contrôlée* status produce wine which is, at its best, distinctly superior to the wines entitled to no more than the Bordeaux appellation. These are Blaye, Bourg and the Premières Côtes de Bordeaux. Their great interest lies in the future: as the demand for good wines has increased, growers have begun to appreciate not only the advantages which can be drawn from giving a 'taste identity' to the wines of an *appellation contrôlée*, but also the possibilities which advertising and marketing an appellation rather than a single property hold out for them. The movement seems likely to grow and is to the advantage of both grower and consumer.

BLAYE

Blaye is a small town which has a fine fortress built in the seventeenth century by Vauban, the French military architect, and a ferry which goes across the Gironde estuary to Lamarque, the village just north of Margaux in the Médoc. The town gives its name to a large wine-producing area situated generally north-east of the town.

The area used to make large quantities of very acid white wines best suited for distilling, and sold these to the distillers and merchants of brandies for their lesser Cognacs. This became illegal after a court decision of 1909 and the vineyard owners had the difficult task of trying to make acceptable dry white table wine from unsuitable grape varieties. For the last 20 years or so most replanting in the area has been in red varieties, usually Merlot, and these are the wines on which the growers place their hopes for the future.

The area is not only a large one, with extensive forests on land which would not qualify for growing wine even if cleared, but has great variety of soil and subsoil. Some of the land which is entitled to make wine with the appellation (usually black, sandy soil ideal for asparagus) is the subject of much debate among the inspectors of the *appellation contrôlée*, who would much prefer to see it condemned to make nothing better than *vin de table* (basic table wine). This restriction of inherited rights is unlikely to occur, but the difficulty of making good wine from such land will probably discourage farmers from replanting, even if it does not spur them on to grub

up their existing vines. This does not mean that some areas do not have excellent soil for growing grapes: the first 5-6 km/3-4 miles inland from the estuary, level with and below Blaye itself, are the best, but not the only areas on which very good wine is made.

Blaye wines have a confusing number of names. It is easier to make sense of the wine labels if you remember that (1) almost all wines with the appellations 'Blaye' or 'Blayais' are white; (2) all wines with the appellation 'Côtes de Blaye' are red; and (3) almost all wines with the more demanding appellation 'Premières Côtes de Blaye' are also red.

Few properties have yet made much of a name for themselves, but we can mention **Château l'Escadre**, a well-kept vineyard in an excellent commune, Cars, which is just outside Blaye. The wines here are vigorous but not elegant.

Further inland, but on land sufficiently hilly to ensure good drainage, is the commune of Berson, also with a number of producers of sound wines. **Château le Chay** is representative of these, with the carefully kept vineyards and tidy cellars which are the hallmark of those properties of the region whose owners have decided to go for quality rather than to attempt to produce huge quantities for sale at low prices.

Of the many *caves coopératives* in the region, that of Générac, about 13 km/8 miles north-east of the town of Blaye, is one that can be relied on for good Premières Côtes de Blaye wine. It is not sold under a château name, but the *cave*'s name is clearly indicated on each bottle.

BOURG

The Bourg appellation is directly south of the region of Blaye and forms a more compact area, not extending so far from the river. The water which forms its western boundary is both the Dordogne and the Gironde (the latter being the estuary of the Dordogne and Garonne rivers), and most of the best growths are within 5 km/3 miles of the river bank although, as in the Médoc, there are low-lying strips of flat alluvial soil which can claim no more than the appellation Bordeaux, since their wine does not have the character of the Bourg appellation.

Bourg lies on the Dordogne and used to be a busy port.
Most of its activity is now centred on the wines which bear its name.

This is a delightful area to explore, with hillier country than almost anywhere else in the Gironde department, and with prehistoric caves (the Grottes de Pair-non-Pair) and quarries in which fossils can be found by those armed with patience and sharp eyesight.

Bourg wines are traditionally slightly coarse, with deep colour and a powerful but not very subtle taste. Unlike Blaye, whose long connection with making cheap white wine for distillation left the buyer with no hint as to the style of wine he might expect to find in a bottle of red wine from the area, Bourg has a tradition of making red wine. Although of variable quality, its local appeal was well-established, its character known. This situation has changed somewhat over the last ten years, for the enterprising local growers had a market research team find out what Bourg represented to the consumer and what changes in style would be appreciated. The general thrust of the report which was finally submitted was to the effect that Bourg was considered a 'rustic' wine, lacking in elegance, and that something smoother, a wine with shoes rather than clogs, would be more appreciated. This, in turn, has encouraged a few changes in vinification and ageing techniques and the wine is now frequently what one would expect the consumer to enjoy: rounder, rarely aggressive and ready to drink earlier. On the whole, the change is probably salutary and certainly this writer cannot hide a sympathy for the appellation, but there are times when a bottle of the old-style robust and powerful Bourg would be welcome.

The proprietors of this appellation can choose between three names for their wine: Bourg, Côtes de Bourg and Bourgeais. The area also makes white wine entitled to the Bourg appellation.

One of the biggest and most distinguished wine-making properties in the region is **Château de**

Barbe, in the commune of Villeneuve, halfway between the towns of Bourg and Blaye. It is a handsome château with a fine tradition. The wines are elegant, with great subtlety of taste, and show well after two years in bottle. Another large property in the Bourg commune is **Château de la Grave**, which makes a quite different wine, with more of the sterner qualities which claret can have. It develops rather more slowly, and has power and concentration.

The commune of Tauriac, in the southern half of the appellation, has a very good *cave coopérative* with the disadvantage of looking like an industrial pile. This is an excellent commune for wine growing and the director of the *cave* ensures that the wines are consistently well made. What is not always clear to the visitor to vineyards is that a producer may have only 1 or 2 hectares and rely on quite another business for his livelihood: the butcher and the plumber may be grape growers when they are not serving the neighbourhood in other ways. For many of these growers, the *cave coopérative* offers a way of ensuring sound vinification under competent direction.

Among the smaller properties **Château Conilh Haut Libarde** is one of the best, producing well-balanced wines with enough backbone to last well and enough complexity to be interesting to taste rather than merely agreeable to drink.

Of the three regions in this section, Bourg is that which has been best able to unite its growers and present a positive approach to marketing wines which do not enjoy the greatest fame.

PREMIÈRES CÔTES DE BORDEAUX

The 'First Hills of Bordeaux' are the vineyards which lie on the right bank of the Garonne and which start opposite Bordeaux to follow the river for some 50 km/30 miles south.

The area produces both red and white wines, but the demands of the market encourage growers to plant red rather than white vines and most of the younger growers are concentrating on making red wine.

This is good grape-growing land, with a solid chalk base and, usually, rich and well-drained soil, benefiting from the hilly character of this part of the Gironde which removes all danger of water damage to the vines. The long, thin area covered by the appellation shares a problem with the Graves, in that the area nearest Bordeaux is also being eroded by the activity of local builders. A further difficulty is that the region is too large and elongated to encourage the sort of unified local effort which has been of such benefit to the growers of Bourg.

Without trying to impose any order on an area which so evidently lacks it, however similar the character of its wines, here are some names which may be encountered and which help to give an idea of why the area is worth exploring.

Yvrac lies in a commune which one truly feels to be in the 'First Hills' of the city of Bordeaux and which has a small airport in the middle of the vines. One of the larger properties, which makes good wine with deep colour, much fruit and some distinction, is **Domaine de Bouteilley**. The owner sells to restaurants throughout France and the wine is usually not expensive.

Langoiran is situated in hills somewhat further from the city of Bordeaux, where it is possible, with a little imagination, to think that the town is far away. The builders are approaching, however, and how long properties like **Château Barreyre** will continue to make wine is much in question. In the meantime an excellent red wine is produced with the subtlety which distinguishes this Premières Côtes de Bordeaux from a basic Bordeaux appellation wine.

About 32 km/20 miles from Bordeaux, a typical property which regularly produces an outstanding wine, one of the best of the large area, is **Château Lamothe**, a substantial vineyard with very big production. This is a wine vinified without any concession to what is regarded by many as a secondary appellation: it is made to show the subtlety as well as the charm which this area can offer. The château is located in the commune of Haux.

François Mauriac, the Nobel Prize-winning writer who came from and wrote about Bordeaux for much of his long life, lived at **Château Malagar**, which is in the very south of the Premières Côtes, about 3 km/2 miles from Langon. There is a plan to open the château to the public, but what concerns us here is that the red wine is excellent, with much fruit and freshness, worth buying even if your interest in French novelists is limited.

BLAYE, BOURG AND THE PREMIÈRES CÔTES DE BORDEAUX

All the wines mentioned here represent good value at the time of writing; few other properties in these areas are sufficiently established to produce first-rate wines regularly.

BORDEAUX AND
BORDEAUX SUPÉRIEUR

In 1986, a shade more than half the red wine with an *appellation contrôlée* made in the Gironde department had the appellation Bordeaux or Bordeaux Supérieur.

Provided that other criteria are respected, any land approved for wine production by the authorities may produce *appellation Bordeaux contrôlée* wine. This applies as much to the most precious plot of St Julien as to the meanest stretch of muddy soil by the side of the Gironde, although the St Julien grower is unlikely to take advantage of this particular possibility, and the grower of grapes on the rich soil by the side of the river may prefer to make a huge quantity of table wine, without any appellation, rather than accept the limitations on quantity per hectare which are imposed on Bordeaux appellation wines.

From this it will be apparent that there is no necessary similarity of soil between one Bordeaux property and another: every single variety of soil existing in the department is used for making the wine and since the soil determines much of the style of a wine, there can be no unity of style within this basic appellation. Indeed, the sheer variety of the origin and style of the wines makes precise comment or valid generalization impossible.

In most areas the grape varieties used are exactly known, as is their age. This is true in many areas where basic Bordeaux wine is made, especially in plantations of clonal selections carried out over the last 10 or 15 years, but it is not at all true in small properties with old vines. It is still not uncommon to find rows of vines planted by someone who has long gone to the cemetery, as the vineyard workers like to say, where different varieties, and even white and red varieties, coexist. A good nurseryman will admit that he is not sure of the identity of some of these vines, and the modest vineyard owner knows no more than that he will be glad when he has sufficient funds to replant with new vines and can be confident that he is not feeding some cuckoo's egg of a variety, useless for the making of wine.

The diversity of treatment lavished on the vine is another source of difference in style. Organic wine growing is impossible in the area because of the weakening of the soil through the unchanging presence of vines, but farming methods do vary considerably. In particular, variations in pruning (to obtain high production of lesser quality or smaller quantities of better wine) have an immediate and appreciable effect on the quality of wine.

Winemaking processes and the nature of the equipment have much to do with style and quality, and vary to an alarming extent. Some growers are still following the precepts of their grandfathers, producing wines with impenetrable colour and a powerful amount of tannin, which will come into their own, if at all, when the maker's newborn grandson eventually celebrates his marriage. Other growers prefer to make wine which is closer to the requirements of the market and are properly equipped to achieve this aim.

The weather, finally, causes greater variation in quality at the level of the basic wines of Bordeaux than for the *Cru Classé*, which can afford to take many expensive decisions (including the rejection of a large part of its harvest) to protect its quality and reputation. It is one of the signs of really fine properties that they produce good wine regularly, great wine at least occasionally. Basic Bordeaux may be excellent in good years, but is unlikely to be better than sound in a poor vintage and can never be great. The range of quality from year to year is substantial and the most intelligent of the growers making traditional Bordeaux sell off their lesser vintages, keeping only the better for a faithful clientele.

What is said above is in no way intended to discourage you from tasting, drinking and buying the basic wines. On the contrary, their sheer variety offers the opportunity of exciting discoveries. When the cork is drawn you may find an excellent bargain, a wine that is not only sound but which expresses, in however modest a way, the pleasures of red Bordeaux. Here are some suggestions which may act as signposts for your own voyage of exploration.

One of the most promising areas to start your search is the area between the Garonne and Dordogne rivers, whose white wines include the Entre Deux Mers. The decline in interest in the slightly sweet white wines which used to be made here encouraged two equally admirable reactions: sharp improvement in the quality of the dry white wine and replanting in red varieties, combined with new

Although machines are used at some properties, most vineyards
in Bordeaux prefer the grapes for quality wines to be hand-picked.

and more efficient methods of grape-growing and winemaking. One such property is **Château Toutigeac**, in Targon, a commune in the middle of the huge tongue of land. The rows of grapes are grown wide apart, the ground between the rows planted in a short grass which allows spraying machines to pass in all weather rather than be bogged down in ploughed soil, and the winemaking equipment is kept in the state of cleanliness that is more normally connected with a dairy than with grape farming. The intended and achieved aim is the production of a wine of good colour, with much fruit on the nose, and an agreeable taste and finish. There is no great complexity of bouquet or taste, but the consumer enjoys an excellent bottle of wine and honour is done to the Bordeaux appellation.

In Vérac, a commune in the area which lies around Fronsac but which has no right to that appellation, there are some excellent small properties. At random, **Clos de Brague** makes a wine in traditional style, which improves with a year or two in bottle (the owner might well claim more), and which offers more complexity and less immediate charm than the

wine from Château Toutigeac described above.

What good wines can be produced from the alluvial soil which makes up so much of the land area in the Gironde is well shown by the small property of **Château Beau Rivage**, which is in the commune of Macau, in the Médoc. The wine has none of the aristocratic qualities of the grander appellation, but it is good, powerful claret, somewhat longer on the palate than either of those mentioned above. Do not confuse this wine with the brand of red Bordeaux which bears a similar name, lacking the vital word 'château'.

A last example will serve to give a hint of the pleasures which can be found within these appellations of Bordeaux and Bordeaux Supérieur. **Château le Dragon** is a property in Caudrot, which is as far from Bordeaux as a wine-producing commune can be, in an area whose semi-sweet white wines have the *appellation contrôlée* Bordeaux St Macaire. The estate is quite large, but the emphasis is very much on quality in obvious terms: trying to make the best wine in a straightforward manner. The success of the attempt can be judged from the wine in bottle.

INDEX

Figures in *italic* refer to captions to illustrations.

ACKNOWLEDGEMENTS
The Publishers thank the following for providing the photographs in
this book:
Ace Photo Library (Adrian Fox) 51, 74; Art Directors Photo Library 8/9;
Antony Blake Photo Library 36, 43, 58/9; Michael Busselle 15, 16, 48/9,
72; Patrick Eager 25 right, 63, 65, 67, 68; Susan Griggs Agency (Adam
Woolfitt) 1, 21, 34/5; Denis Hughes-Gilby 53, 60; Octopus Books Ltd
(Colin Maher) 22, 25 left, 39, 77; Photographers' Library 2/3, 41, 55; Tony
Stone Associates (Richard Passmore) 44; Top Agence (Francois Ducasse)
17, 45, 47, 70/1; Topham Picture Library 46.

Editor: Wendy Lee
Art Editor: Bob Gordon
Designer: Ted Kinsey
Picture Research: Angela Grant

Map Illustrations: Russell Barnett
Grape Illustrations: Nicki Kemball
represented by John Hodgson